A.I. SOLVING EMOTIONAL PROBLEMS:

HOW ARTIFICIAL INTELLIGENCE CAN HELP HUMANS IN EMOTIONAL SITUATIONS AND MAKE BETTER DECISIONS

BY

HENRY E. PARKINS

COPYRIGHT PAGE

TABLE OF CONTENTS

INTRODUCTION

In the vast landscape of technological innovation, the emergence of Artificial Intelligence (A.I.) has sparked a myriad of possibilities and transformations across industries. While much of the focus has been on its applications in streamlining processes, enhancing productivity, and driving efficiency, the realm of emotional support and decision-making has remained largely unexplored until recent years.

The human experience is inherently intertwined with emotions, encompassing a spectrum of joys, sorrows, anxieties, and triumphs. Yet, navigating the complexities of emotional landscapes can be daunting, often presenting challenges that impede our ability to make clear, rational decisions. From the throes of stress and anxiety to the depths of depression, emotional turmoil can significantly impact our well-being and hinder our path to fulfillment.

In the midst of these challenges, Artificial Intelligence emerges as a beacon of hope, offering innovative solutions to address emotional problems and empower individuals to make more informed decisions. The convergence of A.I. and Emotional Intelligence represents a groundbreaking frontier in human-computer interaction, revolutionizing the way we perceive and manage our emotions.

This book, "A.I. Solving Emotional Problems: How Artificial Intelligence Can Help Humans in Emotional Situations and Make Better Decisions," delves into the transformative potential of A.I. in the realm of emotional well-being. Through a comprehensive exploration of cutting-edge technologies, real-world case studies, and ethical considerations, we embark on a journey to unravel the intricate interplay between A.I. and human emotions.

From natural language processing algorithms that provide empathetic support to machine learning models that decipher emotional patterns, the capabilities of A.I. extend far beyond traditional realms of computation. Virtual reality simulations offer immersive environments for emotional healing, while predictive analytics empower individuals to anticipate and navigate emotional challenges with greater resilience.

Yet, as we venture into uncharted territory, we are confronted with a myriad of ethical dilemmas and societal implications. Privacy concerns, algorithmic biases, and the need for cultural sensitivity underscore the imperative for responsible development and deployment of A.I. in emotional support systems.

As we peer into the horizon of possibilities, we envision a future where humans and A.I. collaborate harmoniously to foster emotional resilience, enhance decision-making capabilities, and unlock the full spectrum of human potential. Through empowerment, empathy, and innovation, we strive to harness the transformative power of A.I. to usher in a new era of emotional well-being and collective flourishing.

Join us on this captivating exploration as we illuminate the path towards a more empathetic, emotionally intelligent future—one where A.I. serves as a catalyst for human growth, connection, and fulfillment.

Definition of Emotional Problems

Emotional problems encompass a broad spectrum of psychological challenges that manifest as disruptions in an individual's emotional well-being and ability to cope with daily life stressors. These issues can range from transient feelings of sadness or anxiety to more persistent and debilitating conditions such as depression, chronic stress, or overwhelming grief.

At their core, emotional problems arise from the intricate interplay of biological, psychological, and environmental factors, shaping the way individuals perceive, interpret, and respond to their emotions. Common emotional problems include but are not limited to:

Stress: The body's natural response to perceived threats or demands, which can manifest as physical, emotional, or cognitive symptoms when prolonged or excessive.

Anxiety: A persistent sense of apprehension, worry, or unease, often accompanied by physiological symptoms such as rapid heartbeat, sweating, and muscle tension.

Depression: A mood disorder characterized by persistent feelings of sadness, hopelessness, and disinterest in once-enjoyable activities, which can significantly impair daily functioning and quality of life.

Relationship Challenges: Difficulties in interpersonal connections, communication, and conflict resolution, leading to feelings of loneliness, resentment, or dissatisfaction in personal or professional relationships.

Emotional problems not only impact individual well-being but also influence decision-making processes, cognitive function, and overall life satisfaction. Left unaddressed, they can exacerbate existing challenges, contribute to social isolation, and hinder personal growth and fulfillment.

Recognizing the multifaceted nature of emotional problems is essential for developing effective strategies for intervention, support, and self-care. By fostering awareness, empathy, and resilience, individuals can navigate emotional difficulties with greater clarity, compassion, and adaptive coping mechanisms.

In the context of "A.I. Solving Emotional Problems," understanding the nuances of emotional challenges serves as the foundation for exploring how Artificial Intelligence can offer innovative solutions, empower individuals, and facilitate more informed decision-making in emotional situations. Through a comprehensive understanding of emotional problems, we embark on a journey to unlock the transformative potential of A.I. in promoting emotional well-being and collective flourishing.

Evolution of Artificial Intelligence (A.I.)

The evolution of Artificial Intelligence (A.I.) spans decades of innovation, research, and technological breakthroughs, reshaping the way we perceive and interact with machines. What began as a theoretical concept rooted in the realm of science fiction has burgeoned into a powerful force driving transformative change across industries and disciplines.

Foundations of A.I.: The roots of A.I. can be traced back to the mid-20th century, with pioneers such as Alan Turing laying the groundwork for computational theory and the concept of machine intelligence. Early efforts focused on symbolic reasoning, logic-based systems, and rule-based algorithms, paving the way for early A.I. applications in problem-solving and expert systems.

Machine Learning Revolution:

The advent of machine learning algorithms heralded a new era of A.I. development, characterized by the ability of computers to learn from data and improve performance over time. From neural networks to decision trees, supervised learning to reinforcement learning, machine learning algorithms unlocked unprecedented capabilities in pattern recognition, natural language processing, and predictive analytics.

Deep Learning and Neural Networks:

The rise of deep learning algorithms, particularly convolutional neural networks (CNNs) and recurrent neural networks (RNNs), revolutionized the field of A.I. by enabling the processing of vast amounts of unstructured data with remarkable accuracy and efficiency. Deep learning models have fueled breakthroughs in image recognition, speech synthesis, and language understanding, laying the foundation for A.I. applications in emotional intelligence and human-computer interaction.

A.I. in Emotional Intelligence: As A.I. capabilities continue to advance, researchers and developers are increasingly exploring the intersection of A.I. and Emotional Intelligence (EI). From sentiment analysis to affective computing, A.I. technologies are being harnessed to decode, interpret, and respond to human emotions in real-time. Virtual assistants, chatbots, and emotion recognition systems are among the many A.I. tools designed to provide empathetic support, enhance emotional resilience, and facilitate more meaningful human-machine interactions.

Ethical and Societal Implications: With great power comes great responsibility. As A.I. permeates more aspects of our lives, ethical

considerations surrounding privacy, bias, and accountability have come to the forefront. Ensuring transparent, fair, and inclusive A.I. systems is paramount to mitigating potential risks and safeguarding human well-being in an increasingly digitized world.

As we stand at the cusp of a new frontier in A.I., the possibilities for leveraging A.I. in solving emotional problems and enhancing decision-making capabilities are vast and promising. By tracing the evolution of A.I. and understanding its potential applications in the realm of emotional intelligence, we embark on a journey to harness the transformative power of A.I. to promote emotional well-being and empower individuals to lead more fulfilling lives.

Intersection of A.I. and Emotional Intelligence

The intersection of Artificial Intelligence (A.I.) and Emotional Intelligence (EI) represents a dynamic convergence of cutting-edge technology and profound human understanding. As A.I. continues to evolve, researchers and developers are exploring innovative ways to imbue machines with the capacity to perceive, interpret, and respond to human emotions in a manner that mirrors our own emotional intelligence.

Emotion Recognition and Analysis:

A key area of intersection lies in the realm of emotion recognition and analysis. Through advanced machine learning algorithms and deep learning models, A.I. systems can discern subtle cues in facial expressions, tone of voice, and body language to infer underlying emotions. This capability enables A.I. to gauge emotional states in real-time, providing valuable insights into individuals' mental and emotional well-being.

Empathetic Communication:

A.I. technologies are increasingly being designed to facilitate empathetic communication and support. Natural Language Processing (NLP) algorithms enable A.I. chatbots and virtual assistants to engage in human-like conversations, understand context, and respond with empathy and sensitivity to users' emotional needs. By adapting language and tone to reflect the emotional nuances of human interaction, these A.I. systems foster a sense of connection and understanding, thereby enhancing emotional support and communication.

Personalized Emotional Assistance:

A.I. holds the promise of delivering personalized emotional assistance tailored to individuals' unique needs and preferences. By analyzing vast datasets and learning from user interactions, A.I. algorithms can identify patterns, trends, and triggers associated with specific emotional challenges. This enables the development of targeted interventions, coping strategies, and therapeutic interventions customized to address users' emotional concerns effectively.

Decision-Making Support:

Emotional intelligence plays a pivotal role in decision-making, influencing our ability to assess risks, regulate emotions, and make sound judgments. A.I. systems can augment human decision-making processes by integrating emotional insights and cognitive analysis. Through predictive analytics, sentiment analysis, and behavioral modeling, A.I. helps individuals anticipate the emotional consequences of their decisions, evaluate alternative courses of action, and make more informed choices aligned with their emotional well-being.

Ethical Considerations and Human-Centered Design:

As A.I. technologies become increasingly integrated into emotional support systems, ethical considerations and human-centered design principles are paramount. Safeguarding user privacy, mitigating algorithmic biases, and ensuring transparency and accountability are essential for fostering trust and confidence in A.I.-driven emotional intelligence solutions. By prioritizing ethical practices and human values, we can harness the transformative potential of A.I. to promote emotional well-being and empower individuals to navigate emotional challenges with resilience and compassion.

In exploring the intersection of A.I. and Emotional Intelligence, we embark on a journey to unlock new possibilities for addressing emotional problems, enhancing human-machine interaction, and fostering deeper connections between individuals and technology. Through collaboration, innovation, and empathy, we strive to harness the transformative power of A.I. to create a more emotionally intelligent world where individuals can thrive and make better decisions in the face of emotional complexity.

CHAPTER 1

UNDERSTANDING EMOTIONAL PROBLEMS

Emotional problems represent a multifaceted array of psychological challenges that can significantly impact an individual's well-being, interpersonal relationships, and overall quality of life. Rooted in the intricate interplay of biological, psychological, and environmental factors, these issues manifest in various forms and degrees of severity, each presenting unique obstacles to emotional resilience and adaptive functioning.

Stress: Stress is a natural response to perceived threats or demands, triggering physiological, cognitive, and emotional reactions designed to mobilize resources and cope with challenges. While acute stress can enhance performance and motivation, chronic stress can take a toll on physical health, mental well-being, and interpersonal relationships, contributing to burnout, fatigue, and emotional exhaustion.

Anxiety Disorders: Anxiety disorders encompass a spectrum of conditions characterized by excessive worry, fear, and apprehension in response to real or perceived threats. From generalized anxiety disorder (GAD) to panic disorder, social anxiety disorder, and specific phobias, anxiety disorders can significantly impair daily functioning and undermine individuals' sense of security and self-efficacy.

Depression: Depression is a pervasive mood disorder marked by persistent feelings of sadness, hopelessness, and disinterest in once-enjoyable activities. Beyond emotional distress, depression can manifest in physical symptoms such as fatigue, changes in appetite or sleep patterns, and impaired concentration, posing significant challenges to individuals' ability to function optimally in their personal and professional lives.

Relationship Challenges: Interpersonal relationships play a central role in emotional well-being, providing sources of support, intimacy, and belongingness. However, relationship challenges such as conflicts, communication breakdowns, and interpersonal stressors can strain bonds, erode trust, and foster feelings of loneliness and isolation. Whether in romantic partnerships, familial dynamics, or professional contexts, navigating relational dynamics requires emotional insight, communication skills, and conflict resolution strategies.

Grief and Loss: Grief is a natural response to loss, encompassing a range of emotional, cognitive, and behavioral reactions to the death of a loved one, significant life transitions, or the loss of cherished dreams and aspirations. While grief is a universal experience, its manifestations vary widely across individuals and cultures, reflecting diverse coping mechanisms, cultural norms, and beliefs surrounding death and mourning.

Understanding emotional problems entails recognizing the complex interplay of biological, psychological, social, and environmental factors that shape individuals' emotional experiences and responses to adversity. By fostering empathy, compassion, and resilience, we can cultivate a deeper understanding of emotional challenges and develop effective strategies for intervention, support, and healing.

Types of Emotional Issues

Emotional issues encompass a diverse spectrum of psychological challenges that individuals may encounter throughout their lives. These issues can arise from various sources, including personal experiences, environmental factors, and underlying mental health conditions. Understanding the different types of emotional issues is essential for developing targeted interventions and support strategies. Here are some common types of emotional issues:

Stress: Stress is a natural response to perceived threats or demands, triggering a cascade of physiological and psychological reactions designed to help individuals cope with challenges. However, chronic or excessive stress can lead to physical and emotional exhaustion, impairing cognitive function, sleep patterns, and overall well-being.

Anxiety Disorders: Anxiety disorders are characterized by persistent and excessive worry or fear that is out of proportion to the actual threat. Conditions such as generalized anxiety disorder (GAD), panic disorder, social anxiety disorder, and phobias can significantly interfere with daily functioning, relationships, and quality of life.

Depression: Depression is a mood disorder characterized by persistent feelings of sadness, hopelessness, and disinterest in activities that were once enjoyed. Symptoms may include changes in appetite or sleep patterns, fatigue, difficulty concentrating, and thoughts of self-harm or suicide. Depression can profoundly impact all aspects of life and requires professional intervention for effective management and treatment.

Trauma and Post-Traumatic Stress Disorder (PTSD): Trauma can result from experiencing or witnessing a distressing or life-threatening event, such as physical violence, natural disasters, or military combat. Post-traumatic stress disorder (PTSD) may develop in some

23

individuals following a traumatic experience, leading to intrusive memories, flashbacks, hypervigilance, and avoidance behaviors.

Grief and Loss: Grief is a natural response to the loss of a loved one, significant life changes, or the end of a meaningful relationship. The grieving process may involve a range of emotions, including sadness, anger, guilt, and disbelief, as individuals come to terms with their loss and adjust to a new reality.

Relationship Issues: Interpersonal relationships can be a source of joy and fulfillment, but they can also give rise to emotional challenges and conflicts. Relationship issues may stem from communication difficulties, trust issues, conflicting values or priorities, and unresolved conflicts, leading to feelings of loneliness, resentment, or dissatisfaction.

Self-Esteem and Body Image Concerns: Low self-esteem and negative body image can profoundly impact individuals' emotional well-being and self-perception. These issues may arise from societal pressures, unrealistic beauty standards, past traumas, or negative self-talk, contributing to feelings of inadequacy, shame, and self-doubt.

Addiction and Substance Abuse:

Addiction and substance abuse disorders are complex emotional issues characterized by compulsive behaviors and an inability to control substance use despite negative consequences. Substance abuse can serve as a coping mechanism for underlying emotional pain, trauma, or stress, exacerbating mental health issues and disrupting relationships and daily functioning.

Recognizing and addressing emotional issues requires a comprehensive understanding of the underlying factors contributing to individuals' emotional distress. By leveraging the capabilities of Artificial Intelligence (A.I.), we can develop innovative solutions and support systems to assist individuals in managing their emotional challenges, making better decisions, and fostering greater emotional resilience and well-being.

Stress

Stress is a ubiquitous aspect of the human experience, affecting individuals of all ages, backgrounds, and circumstances. It is a natural physiological response to perceived threats or demands, triggering a complex cascade of hormonal and neurological reactions designed to mobilize resources and cope with challenges.

Nature of Stress: Stress can manifest in various forms, ranging from everyday stressors such as work deadlines, financial pressures, and relationship conflicts to major life events such as moving, job loss, or illness. While acute stress can be adaptive, motivating individuals to take action and respond to immediate threats, chronic or excessive stress can have detrimental effects on physical health, mental well-being, and overall quality of life.

Physiological Responses: When faced with stress, the body initiates a series of physiological responses known as the "fight-or-flight" response. This includes the release of stress hormones such as cortisol and adrenaline, which increase heart rate, elevate blood pressure, and sharpen focus in preparation for action. While these responses can be beneficial in short bursts, prolonged activation of the stress response can lead to a range of health problems, including cardiovascular disease, immune system suppression, and gastrointestinal disorders.

Psychological Impact:

Chronic stress can take a toll on mental health, contributing to symptoms of anxiety, depression, and burnout. Persistent feelings of overwhelm, irritability, and fatigue may accompany chronic stress, making it difficult for individuals to cope with daily responsibilities and maintain a sense of balance and well-being. Stress can also impair cognitive function, memory, and decision-making abilities, affecting performance at work, school, and in interpersonal relationships.

Coping Strategies:

Effective stress management involves developing healthy coping strategies to mitigate the impact of stress on mind and body. This may include practicing relaxation techniques such as deep breathing, mindfulness meditation, or progressive muscle relaxation. Engaging in regular physical activity, maintaining a balanced diet, and prioritizing adequate sleep are also important for supporting overall resilience and well-being. Additionally, seeking social support, setting realistic goals, and practicing self-care can help individuals navigate stressful situations more effectively.

A.I. Solutions for Stress:

Artificial Intelligence (A.I.) holds promise in providing innovative solutions for stress management and emotional support. A.I.-powered applications such as virtual assistants, mindfulness meditation apps, and stress tracking tools can offer personalized interventions, actionable insights, and real-time support to help individuals identify triggers, manage stressors, and cultivate greater resilience in the face of adversity. By leveraging A.I. technologies, individuals can access tailored resources and strategies to cope with stress more effectively and make healthier decisions in emotional situations.

Understanding the nature of stress and its impact on emotional well-being is essential for developing effective strategies for stress management and resilience-building.

By integrating A.I. solutions into the realm of stress management, we can empower individuals to navigate life's challenges with greater ease, make informed decisions, and cultivate a sense of balance and well-being amidst the complexities of modern life.

Anxiety

Anxiety is a pervasive emotional issue that affects millions of individuals worldwide, ranging from occasional feelings of unease to debilitating episodes of panic and fear. It is characterized by excessive worry, apprehension, and nervousness in response to real or perceived threats, often leading to significant distress and impairment in daily functioning.

Nature of Anxiety: Anxiety is a natural response to stressors and challenges in life, serving as a protective mechanism designed to alert individuals to potential danger and motivate adaptive behaviors. However, when anxiety becomes disproportionate to the actual threat or persists beyond the triggering event, it can interfere with various aspects

of life, including work, relationships, and overall well-being.

Types of Anxiety Disorders:

Anxiety disorders encompass a spectrum of conditions characterized by persistent and excessive anxiety that significantly disrupts daily life. Common types of anxiety disorders include:

a. Generalized Anxiety Disorder (GAD): Individuals with GAD experience chronic and excessive worry about various aspects of life, such as work, health, relationships, and finances, even when there is little or no apparent reason for concern.

b. Panic Disorder: Panic disorder is characterized by recurrent and unexpected panic attacks, which are intense periods of fear or discomfort accompanied by physical symptoms such as rapid heartbeat, sweating, trembling, and shortness of breath.

c. Social Anxiety Disorder: Social anxiety disorder involves an intense fear of social situations and scrutiny by others, leading to avoidance of social interactions,

30

public speaking, and performance situations.

d. Specific Phobias: Specific phobias are characterized by irrational and intense fears of specific objects or situations, such as heights, flying, spiders, or enclosed spaces, leading to avoidance behaviors and significant distress when confronted with the feared stimulus.

Impact of Anxiety: Anxiety can have profound effects on individuals' emotional, cognitive, and physical well-being. Persistent anxiety can lead to feelings of restlessness, irritability, difficulty concentrating, and sleep disturbances, impairing performance at work or school and straining interpersonal relationships. Chronic anxiety is also associated with an increased risk of other mental health conditions, such as depression, substance abuse, and eating disorders.

Treatment and Management: Effective treatment for anxiety often involves a combination of psychotherapy, medication, lifestyle modifications, and stress management techniques. Cognitive-behavioral therapy (CBT) is one of the most

widely used psychotherapeutic approaches for anxiety disorders, helping individuals identify and challenge negative thought patterns, develop coping strategies, and gradually confront feared situations. Medications such as selective serotonin reuptake inhibitors (SSRIs) and benzodiazepines may be prescribed to alleviate symptoms of anxiety and promote relaxation in some cases. Additionally, lifestyle modifications such as regular exercise, relaxation techniques, mindfulness meditation, and adequate sleep can help individuals manage anxiety and promote overall well-being.

A.I. Solutions for Anxiety: Artificial Intelligence (A.I.) holds promise in providing innovative solutions for anxiety management and support. A.I.-powered applications such as chatbots, virtual therapists, and anxiety tracking tools can offer personalized interventions, real-time support, and actionable insights to help individuals identify triggers, challenge distorted thinking patterns, and develop coping strategies for managing anxiety symptoms. By leveraging A.I. technologies, individuals can access tailored resources

and support to navigate anxiety more effectively, make healthier decisions in emotional situations, and enhance overall emotional well-being.

Understanding the nature of anxiety and its impact on individuals' lives is essential for developing effective strategies for anxiety management and resilience-building. By integrating A.I. solutions into the realm of anxiety management, we can empower individuals to cope with anxiety more effectively, navigate life's challenges with greater ease, and cultivate a sense of calm and balance amidst the complexities of modern life.

Depression:

Depression is a pervasive and debilitating mood disorder that affects millions of individuals worldwide, profoundly impacting their emotional well-being, relationships, and overall quality of life. Characterized by persistent feelings of sadness, hopelessness, and disinterest in once-enjoyable activities, depression can have far-reaching consequences and require comprehensive interventions for effective management and treatment.

Nature of Depression: Depression is more than just feeling sad or down; it is a complex and multifaceted condition that affects individuals on emotional, cognitive, and physical levels. While everyone experiences periods of sadness or low mood from time to time, depression involves persistent and pervasive symptoms that significantly impair functioning and quality of life.

Symptoms of Depression: Symptoms of depression can vary widely among individuals but may include:

a. Persistent feelings of sadness, emptiness, or hopelessness b. Loss of interest or pleasure in activities once enjoyed c. Changes in appetite or weight d. Insomnia or oversleeping e. Fatigue or loss of energy f. Feelings of worthlessness or excessive guilt g. Difficulty concentrating or making decisions h. Thoughts of death or suicide

Types of Depression: Depression encompasses various forms and presentations, including:

a. Major Depressive Disorder (MDD): MDD is characterized by persistent and severe depressive symptoms that interfere with daily functioning and last for at least two weeks or longer.

b. Persistent Depressive Disorder (PDD): PDD, formerly known as dysthymia, involves chronic depressive symptoms that persist for at least two years, often fluctuating in intensity but rarely remitting completely.

c. Seasonal Affective Disorder (SAD): SAD is a type of depression that occurs seasonally, typically during the winter months when daylight hours are shorter. Symptoms may include fatigue, changes in appetite, and social withdrawal.

d. Postpartum Depression: Postpartum depression occurs in new mothers following childbirth and is characterized by intense feelings of sadness, anxiety, and exhaustion. It can interfere with bonding with the newborn and affect the mother's ability to care for herself and her baby.

Risk Factors and Causes:

Depression can arise from a complex

interplay of genetic, biological, environmental, and psychological factors. While anyone can experience depression, certain risk factors may increase susceptibility, including a family history of depression, traumatic life events, chronic stress, medical conditions, substance abuse, and certain medications.

Treatment and Management:

Effective treatment for depression often involves a combination of psychotherapy, medication, lifestyle modifications, and support from healthcare professionals and loved ones. Psychotherapy, particularly cognitive-behavioral therapy (CBT) and interpersonal therapy (IPT), can help individuals identify and challenge negative thought patterns, develop coping strategies, and improve interpersonal relationships. Antidepressant medications, such as selective serotonin reuptake inhibitors (SSRIs) and serotonin-norepinephrine reuptake inhibitors (SNRIs), may be prescribed to alleviate symptoms and restore chemical imbalances in the brain. Additionally, lifestyle modifications such as regular exercise, healthy diet, adequate sleep, and stress management techniques can play a crucial role in managing depression and promoting overall well-being.

A.I. Solutions for Depression:

Artificial Intelligence (A.I.) holds promise in providing innovative solutions for depression management and support. A.I.-powered applications such as chatbots, virtual therapists, and mood tracking tools can offer personalized interventions, real-time support, and actionable insights to help individuals manage depressive symptoms, identify triggers, and develop coping strategies for improving mood and emotional well-being. By leveraging A.I. technologies, individuals can access tailored resources and support to navigate depression more effectively, make healthier decisions in emotional situations, and enhance overall emotional resilience and recovery.

Understanding the nature of depression and its impact on individuals' lives is essential for developing effective strategies for depression management and resilience-building. By integrating A.I. solutions into the realm of depression management, we can empower individuals to cope with depression more effectively, navigate life's challenges with greater ease, and cultivate a sense of hope and healing amidst the complexities of mental health.

Relationship Challenges

Relationships are fundamental to human experience, providing avenues for connection, support, and personal growth. However, navigating the complexities of interpersonal dynamics can present numerous challenges and obstacles that require empathy, communication, and resilience to overcome. Relationship challenges encompass a wide range of issues that can strain bonds, erode trust, and impact individuals' emotional well-being and satisfaction in their relationships.

Communication Breakdown:

Effective communication is the cornerstone of healthy relationships, allowing individuals to express their needs, feelings, and boundaries openly and honestly. Communication breakdowns can occur when there is a lack of clarity, understanding, or empathy in interpersonal interactions, leading to misunderstandings, conflicts, and resentment.

Conflict Resolution: Conflict is a natural and inevitable part of any relationship, arising from differences in values, beliefs, priorities, and expectations. However, unresolved conflicts can escalate into resentment, hostility, and emotional distance if not addressed constructively. Effective conflict resolution involves active listening, empathy, compromise, and a willingness to understand and respect each other's perspectives.

Trust Issues: Trust forms the foundation of healthy relationships, fostering feelings of security, intimacy, and mutual respect. Trust issues can arise from past betrayals, breaches of confidentiality, or inconsistencies in behavior, leading to feelings of suspicion, insecurity, and doubt. Rebuilding trust requires transparency, consistency, and accountability in actions and words over time.

Intimacy and Connection: Intimacy encompasses emotional closeness, vulnerability, and authenticity in

relationships, fostering feelings of connection and mutual understanding. Challenges with intimacy may stem from fear of rejection, past trauma, or communication barriers, leading to feelings of loneliness, disconnection, or emotional distance.

Boundary Setting:

Establishing and maintaining healthy boundaries is essential for preserving individual autonomy, self-respect, and emotional well-being within relationships. Boundary issues may arise when individuals struggle to assert their needs, assertiveness, or when there is a lack of respect for personal boundaries, leading to feelings of resentment, power struggles, or codependency.

Cultural and Interpersonal Differences:

Cultural and interpersonal differences can enrich relationships by offering diverse perspectives, values, and experiences. However, navigating cultural and interpersonal differences requires empathy, curiosity, and a willingness to learn and adapt to each other's backgrounds and preferences.

Life Transitions and Stressors:

Major life transitions, such as moving, career changes, starting a family, or coping with illness, can strain relationships and disrupt established routines and dynamics. Coping with stressors and transitions requires effective communication, support, and flexibility to adapt to changing circumstances and needs.

Artificial Intelligence (A.I.) holds promise in addressing relationship challenges by providing innovative solutions and support systems to assist individuals in navigating interpersonal dynamics and fostering healthier, more fulfilling connections. A.I.-powered applications such as relationship coaching, communication tools, and conflict resolution platforms can offer personalized insights, actionable strategies, and real-time support to help individuals understand, navigate, and overcome relationship challenges effectively. By leveraging A.I. technologies, individuals can enhance their emotional intelligence, communication skills, and relationship resilience, fostering deeper connections and mutual understanding in their interpersonal interactions.

The Impact of Emotional Problems on Decision-Making

Emotional problems, such as stress, anxiety, depression, and relationship challenges, can exert a profound influence on individuals' decision-making processes, often clouding judgment, impairing cognitive function, and hindering the ability to weigh options rationally. The interplay between emotions and decision-making is complex and multifaceted, encompassing a range of cognitive, affective, and behavioral factors that shape the choices individuals make in various contexts of their lives.

Cognitive Biases: Emotional problems can give rise to cognitive biases systematic errors in thinking—that distort perception, interpretation, and evaluation of information. For instance, individuals experiencing anxiety may be prone to catastrophic thinking, overestimating the likelihood of negative outcomes and underestimating their ability to cope with challenges. Similarly, depression may lead to cognitive distortions such as all-or-nothing thinking, where individuals perceive situations in overly simplistic terms, discounting nuances and alternative perspectives.

Risk Aversion and Avoidance Behavior:

Emotional problems often heighten sensitivity to perceived threats and uncertainties, leading individuals to adopt risk-averse or avoidance behaviors in decision-making. For example, individuals experiencing anxiety may avoid taking calculated risks or pursuing opportunities for growth and advancement due to fear of failure or rejection. Similarly, depression may sap motivation and initiative, causing individuals to withdraw from decision-making altogether and passively accept the status quo.

Impaired Problem-Solving Skills:

Emotional problems can impair individuals' ability to engage in effective problem-solving and decision-making strategies. Chronic stress, for instance, can compromise working memory, attentional control, and cognitive flexibility, making it difficult to generate and evaluate alternative solutions to complex problems.

Likewise, anxiety and depression may diminish cognitive resources available for decision-making, leading to indecisiveness, rumination, and analysis paralysis.

Interpersonal Dynamics and Conflict Resolution:

Emotional problems can escalate interpersonal conflicts and complicate resolution efforts, particularly in intimate relationships, professional settings, and collaborative environments. Communication breakdowns, mistrust, and emotional reactivity may exacerbate tensions and impede constructive dialogue, making it challenging to find mutually satisfactory solutions and reach consensus.

Impulsivity and Emotional Reactivity:

Emotional problems can heighten impulsivity and emotional reactivity, leading individuals to make hasty decisions based on immediate gratification or short-term relief from distress. For example, individuals experiencing intense emotions such as anger or frustration may act impulsively without considering long-term consequences or weighing alternative courses of action, increasing the likelihood of regrettable outcomes.

A.I. Solutions for Enhancing Decision-Making in Emotional Situations:

Artificial Intelligence (A.I.) holds promise in mitigating the impact of emotional problems on decision-making by providing innovative solutions and support systems that augment individuals' cognitive and emotional capacities. A.I.-powered decision support tools, cognitive behavioral therapy (CBT) apps, and emotion regulation training programs can offer personalized insights, evidence-based interventions, and real-time feedback to help individuals navigate emotional situations more effectively and make better decisions aligned with their goals and values.

By understanding the complex interplay between emotional problems and decision-making, and by leveraging the transformative potential of A.I., individuals can cultivate greater self-awareness, emotional regulation, and adaptive coping strategies to navigate life's challenges with resilience and clarity of mind. Through collaboration, innovation, and empathy, we can harness the power of A.I. to empower individuals to make more informed decisions, foster emotional well-being, and achieve greater fulfillment in their lives.

CHAPTER 2

A.I. TECHNOLOGIES FOR EMOTIONAL PROBLEM SOLVING

Artificial Intelligence (A.I.) technologies have emerged as powerful tools for addressing emotional problems and enhancing individuals' ability to navigate emotional situations with greater resilience and insight. By leveraging advanced algorithms, data analytics, and machine learning techniques, A.I. offers innovative solutions that augment human capacities for emotional understanding, regulation, and decision-making. Here are some key A.I. technologies for emotional problem solving:

Emotion Recognition Systems:

Emotion recognition systems utilize machine learning algorithms to analyze facial expressions, vocal intonations, and physiological signals to infer individuals' emotional states in real-time. By detecting subtle cues and patterns associated with different emotions, these systems can provide valuable insights into individuals' emotional well-being and facilitate more empathetic and responsive interactions in various contexts, such as customer service, healthcare, and education.

Sentiment Analysis:

Sentiment analysis algorithms analyze textual data, such as social media posts, customer reviews, and online discussions, to identify and quantify the emotional tone and sentiment expressed by users. By parsing and categorizing language patterns and expressions, sentiment analysis tools can help organizations and individuals gauge public opinion, monitor brand perception, and identify emerging trends and issues that may impact emotional well-being and decision-making.

Virtual Mental Health Assistants:

Virtual mental health assistants, powered by natural language processing (NLP) and machine learning algorithms, provide personalized support and guidance to individuals experiencing emotional distress or mental health challenges. These virtual assistants offer empathetic listening, psychoeducation, coping strategies, and referrals to professional services, enabling users to access timely and confidential support in a convenient and accessible format.

Affective Computing:

Affective computing technologies aim to imbue computers and digital interfaces with the ability to recognize, interpret, and respond to human emotions in naturalistic ways. By integrating emotion recognition, natural language processing, and affective feedback mechanisms, affective computing systems can enhance human-computer interaction, facilitate more empathetic and engaging user experiences, and support emotional well-being in diverse applications, such as virtual reality, gaming, and assistive technologies.

Emotionally Intelligent Chatbots:

Emotionally intelligent chatbots leverage natural language understanding and sentiment analysis to engage users in empathetic and responsive conversations, offering emotional support, guidance, and encouragement in times of need. By detecting and responding to users' emotional cues and context, these chatbots can simulate human-like interactions, build rapport, and foster trust and emotional connection with users, enhancing their emotional resilience and well-being.

Personalized Intervention and Feedback Systems:

Personalized intervention and feedback systems use data analytics and machine learning algorithms to identify individuals' unique emotional patterns, triggers, and coping strategies, and deliver targeted interventions and feedback to support emotional regulation and well-being. By tailoring interventions to individuals' specific needs, preferences, and contexts, these systems empower users to develop self-awareness, self-regulation, and adaptive coping skills to manage emotional challenges effectively.

By harnessing the capabilities of A.I. technologies for emotional problem solving, individuals, organizations, and societies can unlock new opportunities to promote emotional well-being, enhance decision-making, and foster greater empathy, resilience, and connection in the digital age. As we continue to innovate and integrate A.I. solutions into our lives, we have the potential to transform how we understand, navigate, and respond to the complex and nuanced landscape of human emotions and experiences.

Natural Language Processing (NLP) in Emotional Support

Natural Language Processing (NLP) is a branch of artificial intelligence that focuses on the interaction between computers and human language. In the realm of emotional support, NLP plays a pivotal role in facilitating empathetic communication, understanding emotional cues, and providing personalized assistance to individuals navigating emotional challenges. Here's how NLP is revolutionizing emotional support and enhancing decision-making in the context of the book "A.I. Solving Emotional Problems":

Emotion Recognition and Understanding: NLP algorithms analyze textual data, such as chat logs, emails, and social media posts, to detect and interpret emotional cues expressed in

language. By identifying keywords, linguistic patterns, and sentiment indicators, NLP models can infer individuals' emotional states, attitudes, and concerns, enabling more nuanced and empathetic responses from A.I.-powered support systems.

Contextual Understanding and Response Generation: NLP models are capable of understanding context and generating contextually appropriate responses to individuals' emotional queries and expressions. By leveraging techniques such as contextual embedding and conversational context tracking, NLP-powered chatbots and virtual assistants can maintain coherent and engaging dialogues, anticipate users' needs, and provide relevant information, resources, and support tailored to their emotional well-being.

Empathetic Communication and Language Generation: NLP technologies enable A.I. systems to emulate human-like communication styles, tone, and empathy in interactions with users seeking emotional support. Through

sentiment analysis, tone detection, and emotion-aware language generation, NLP-powered chatbots and virtual assistants can adapt their language and responses to reflect users' emotional states and foster a sense of understanding, validation, and connection in the support-seeking process.

Personalized Intervention and Feedback:

NLP-based systems can analyze users' language patterns, emotional triggers, and coping strategies to deliver personalized interventions and feedback aimed at promoting emotional resilience and well-being. By tracking users' emotional progress over time and identifying trends and patterns in their emotional expression, NLP-powered support systems can offer targeted suggestions, coping techniques, and self-care strategies tailored to individuals' unique needs and preferences.

Ethical Considerations and Privacy Protection:

In the context of emotional support, NLP technologies must uphold ethical standards and prioritize user privacy and confidentiality. By implementing robust data encryption, anonymization techniques, and transparent data policies, NLP-powered support systems can safeguard users' sensitive information and foster trust and confidence in the A.I.-human interaction. Additionally, ensuring accountability, transparency, and user consent in the collection and use of emotional data is essential for maintaining ethical standards and respecting individuals' autonomy and dignity.

In summary, NLP plays a crucial role in revolutionizing emotional support and empowering individuals to navigate emotional challenges with greater resilience, insight, and connection. By leveraging the capabilities of NLP-powered A.I. systems, we can enhance decision-making, foster empathy, and promote emotional well-being in the digital age, paving the way for a more compassionate and inclusive society where individuals can thrive and make better decisions in emotional situations.

Chatbots and Virtual Assistants

Chatbots and virtual assistants represent cutting-edge applications of artificial intelligence (A.I.) that hold tremendous potential for providing support, guidance, and intervention in emotional situations, while also aiding individuals in making better decisions. These digital companions leverage sophisticated algorithms and natural language processing (NLP) capabilities to engage users in meaningful conversations, offer empathetic responses, and deliver personalized assistance tailored to individuals' emotional needs. Here's how chatbots and virtual assistants contribute to the book's theme, "A.I. Solving Emotional Problems":

Accessible Emotional Support:

Chatbots and virtual assistants offer accessible and convenient channels for individuals to seek emotional support and guidance anytime, anywhere. Whether through messaging platforms, mobile apps, or web interfaces, these A.I.-powered companions provide a non-judgmental space for users to express their feelings, share their concerns, and receive empathetic responses and coping strategies in real-time.

Empathetic Communication:

Chatbots and virtual assistants are designed to emulate human-like communication styles, tone, and empathy in interactions with users. Through sentiment analysis, emotion recognition, and language generation techniques, these A.I. systems can interpret users' emotional cues, adapt their responses accordingly, and foster a sense of understanding, validation, and connection in the support-seeking process.

Personalized Assistance and Intervention:

Chatbots and virtual assistants leverage machine learning algorithms to analyze users' language patterns, emotional triggers, and coping strategies, enabling them to deliver personalized assistance and interventions tailored to individuals' unique needs and preferences. By tracking users' emotional progress over time and identifying trends and patterns in their emotional expression, these A.I. systems can offer targeted suggestions, coping techniques, and self-care strategies to support emotional resilience and well-being.

24/7 Availability and Responsiveness:

Unlike traditional forms of support, chatbots and virtual assistants are available 24/7 and can respond to users' queries and concerns instantaneously. This round-the-clock availability ensures that individuals have access to emotional support and guidance whenever they need it, without the constraints of time or location, thereby reducing barriers to seeking help and promoting early intervention in emotional crises.

Anonymity and Confidentiality:

Chatbots and virtual assistants provide a safe and confidential space for individuals to express themselves without fear of judgment or stigma. By maintaining user anonymity and confidentiality, these A.I. systems create a trust-based environment where users feel comfortable sharing their deepest thoughts, emotions, and vulnerabilities, fostering a sense of empowerment and agency in managing their emotional well-being.

Integration with Mental Health Services:

Chatbots and virtual assistants can complement traditional mental health services by providing triage, screening, and early intervention for individuals experiencing emotional distress or mental health challenges. Through seamless integration with teletherapy platforms, crisis hotlines, and mental health resources, these A.I. systems can facilitate referrals to professional services and support networks, ensuring that individuals receive the appropriate care and assistance they need to address their emotional concerns effectively.

In summary, chatbots and virtual assistants represent powerful tools for addressing emotional problems, enhancing decision-making, and promoting emotional well-being in the digital age. By harnessing the capabilities of artificial intelligence, we can empower individuals to navigate emotional situations with greater resilience, insight, and support, fostering a more compassionate and inclusive society where everyone has the resources and tools they need to thrive emotionally and make better decisions in their lives.

Sentiment Analysis

Sentiment analysis is a powerful application of artificial intelligence (A.I.) that involves the automated extraction, analysis, and interpretation of emotional cues and attitudes expressed in textual data. In the context of the book title "A.I. Solving Emotional Problems: How Artificial Intelligence Can Help Humans in Emotional Situations and Make Better Decisions," sentiment analysis plays a pivotal role in understanding and addressing emotional challenges, guiding decision-making processes, and enhancing emotional well-being. Here's how sentiment analysis contributes to the book's theme:

Emotion Detection and Classification: Sentiment analysis algorithms analyze textual data, such as social media posts, customer reviews, and online discussions, to detect and classify the emotional tone and sentiment expressed by users. By identifying keywords, linguistic patterns, and context

clues, sentiment analysis models can distinguish between positive, negative, and neutral sentiments, providing valuable insights into individuals' emotional states and perceptions.

Understanding User Feedback and Sentiment: Sentiment analysis helps organizations and individuals gauge public opinion, monitor brand perception, and identify emerging trends and issues that may impact emotional well-being and decision-making. By analyzing user feedback and sentiment across various channels and platforms, such as product reviews, social media mentions, and customer surveys, sentiment analysis enables stakeholders to assess sentiment trends, sentiment polarity, and sentiment intensity, informing strategic decisions and interventions.

Real-Time Monitoring and Intervention: Sentiment analysis enables real-time monitoring of emotional dynamics and sentiment shifts in response to evolving events, trends, and conversations. By leveraging natural language processing (NLP) techniques and machine learning algorithms, sentiment analysis tools can track changes in sentiment patterns, detect outliers and anomalies, and alert stakeholders to emerging issues or crises that require timely intervention and response.

Personalized Recommendations and Interventions:

Sentiment analysis can inform the development of personalized recommendations and interventions aimed at addressing individuals' emotional needs and preferences. By analyzing users' sentiment signals, emotional triggers, and engagement patterns, sentiment analysis algorithms can tailor content, products, and services to match users' emotional states and interests, enhancing user satisfaction, engagement, and emotional well-being.

Ethical Considerations and Privacy Protection:

In the context of sentiment analysis, it is essential to uphold ethical standards and prioritize user privacy and confidentiality. By implementing robust data encryption, anonymization techniques, and transparent data policies, sentiment analysis platforms can safeguard users' sensitive information and foster trust and confidence in the A.I.-human interaction. Additionally, ensuring accountability, transparency, and user consent in the collection and use of sentiment data is crucial for maintaining ethical standards and respecting individuals' autonomy and dignity.

In summary, sentiment analysis serves as a valuable tool for understanding, analyzing, and addressing emotional problems, guiding decision-making processes, and promoting emotional well-being in the digital age. By leveraging the capabilities of sentiment analysis, we can empower individuals, organizations, and societies to navigate emotional situations with greater insight, empathy, and resilience, fostering a more compassionate and inclusive world where everyone's emotional needs are understood, respected, and addressed.

Machine Learning Algorithms for Emotional Insight

Machine learning algorithms play a crucial role in extracting meaningful insights from data and providing valuable support in addressing emotional problems. In the context of the book title "A.I. Solving Emotional Problems: How Artificial Intelligence Can Help Humans in Emotional Situations and Make Better Decisions," machine learning algorithms offer innovative solutions for understanding, managing, and responding to emotional challenges. Here's how machine learning algorithms contribute to emotional insight:

Emotion Recognition: Machine learning algorithms, particularly those in the field of computer vision and natural language processing (NLP), enable the recognition and interpretation of emotional cues expressed through facial expressions, voice tone, and textual language. By analyzing patterns and features associated with different emotions, machine learning models can accurately classify and understand individuals' emotional states, providing valuable insights into their emotional well-being and needs.

Sentiment Analysis: Machine learning algorithms power sentiment analysis techniques that analyze text data to determine the sentiment or emotional

tone conveyed within it. Through the analysis of linguistic patterns, keywords, and context, sentiment analysis algorithms can identify and categorize text as positive, negative, or neutral sentiment, enabling organizations and individuals to gauge public opinion, monitor brand perception, and identify emotional trends and patterns.

Personalized Recommendation Systems:

Machine learning algorithms drive personalized recommendation systems that leverage individuals' emotional and behavioral data to deliver tailored content, products, and services. By analyzing users' past interactions, preferences, and emotional responses, recommendation systems can predict and recommend items that match users' interests, preferences, and emotional states, enhancing user engagement, satisfaction, and emotional well-being.

Emotion-aware Virtual Assistants and Chatbots: Machine learning algorithms power emotion-aware virtual assistants and chatbots that engage users in empathetic and responsive conversations, offering emotional support, guidance, and intervention. By analyzing users' language patterns, emotional cues, and contextual cues, these A.I. systems can adapt their responses and interactions to reflect users' emotional states and needs, fostering a sense of understanding, validation, and connection in the support-seeking process.

Predictive Analytics for Emotional Trends:

Machine learning algorithms enable predictive analytics techniques that forecast emotional trends and patterns based on historical data and contextual factors. By analyzing large datasets of emotional signals and events, predictive analytics models can identify correlations, trends, and predictive patterns that inform decision-making, intervention strategies, and resource allocation in addressing emotional challenges and promoting emotional well-being.

Ethical Considerations and Bias Mitigation:

In the development and deployment of machine learning algorithms for emotional insight, it is essential to address ethical considerations and mitigate biases that may impact the accuracy, fairness, and inclusivity of algorithmic predictions and recommendations. By implementing fairness-aware algorithms, transparency measures, and bias mitigation strategies, developers can ensure that machine learning algorithms uphold ethical standards, respect individuals' autonomy and dignity, and foster trust and confidence in the A.I.-human interaction.

In summary, machine learning algorithms offer powerful tools for gaining insights into emotional states, patterns, and trends, guiding decision-making processes, and promoting emotional well-being in the digital age. By leveraging the capabilities of machine learning, we can enhance our understanding of emotional problems, develop more effective interventions, and create supportive environments that empower individuals to navigate emotional situations with greater insight, resilience, and empathy.

Predictive Analytics

Predictive analytics is a powerful application of artificial intelligence (A.I.) that involves analyzing historical data and identifying patterns, trends, and correlations to make predictions about future events or behaviors. In the context of the book title "A.I. Solving Emotional Problems: How Artificial Intelligence Can Help Humans in Emotional Situations and Make Better Decisions," predictive analytics offers innovative solutions for understanding, managing, and responding to emotional challenges. Here's how predictive analytics contributes to the book's theme:

Emotional Trend Forecasting:
Predictive analytics algorithms analyze large datasets of emotional signals, behaviors, and events to identify trends and patterns in emotional states and responses over time. By examining historical data and contextual factors, predictive analytics models can forecast future emotional trends, anticipate shifts in sentiment, and identify emerging emotional issues or crises that may require intervention and response.

Risk Prediction and Early Intervention: Predictive analytics enables the identification of individuals at risk of experiencing emotional distress or

mental health challenges based on their historical behavior, demographic characteristics, and contextual factors. By leveraging machine learning algorithms, predictive analytics models can predict the likelihood of individuals developing emotional problems or exhibiting maladaptive behaviors, enabling early intervention and targeted support to prevent escalation and promote emotional well-being.

Personalized Intervention Strategies: Predictive analytics drives the development of personalized intervention strategies tailored to individuals' unique needs, preferences, and risk profiles. By analyzing individuals' historical data and emotional trajectories, predictive analytics models can identify effective intervention strategies, coping mechanisms, and support resources that are most likely to resonate with individuals and facilitate positive emotional outcomes.

Resource Allocation and Service Planning: Predictive analytics informs resource allocation and service planning efforts in addressing emotional problems

and promoting emotional well-being. By analyzing population-level data and demand patterns, predictive analytics models can optimize the allocation of mental health resources, intervention programs, and support services to areas and populations with the greatest need, ensuring that resources are allocated efficiently and equitably to meet the diverse needs of individuals and communities.

Continuous Monitoring and Evaluation: Predictive analytics enables continuous monitoring and evaluation of emotional well-being initiatives and intervention programs to assess their effectiveness, identify areas for improvement, and optimize resource allocation and service delivery. By analyzing outcome data and performance metrics, predictive analytics models can evaluate the impact of interventions on individuals' emotional outcomes, identify best practices, and inform evidence-based decision-making in emotional support and intervention efforts.

Ethical Considerations and Privacy Protection: In the development and deployment of predictive analytics for emotional insight, it is essential to address ethical considerations and prioritize user privacy and confidentiality. By implementing robust data anonymization techniques, privacy-preserving algorithms, and transparent data governance policies, predictive analytics platforms can safeguard individuals' sensitive information and foster trust and confidence in the A.I.-human interaction. Additionally, ensuring accountability, transparency, and user consent in the collection and use of emotional data is crucial for maintaining ethical standards and respecting individuals' autonomy and dignity.

In summary, predictive analytics offers valuable insights into emotional trends, behaviors, and outcomes, guiding decision-making processes, and promoting emotional well-being in the digital age. By leveraging the capabilities of predictive analytics, we can enhance our understanding of emotional problems, develop more effective interventions, and create supportive environments that empower individuals to navigate emotional situations with greater insight, resilience, and empathy.

Behavioral Analysis

Behavioral analysis is a fundamental aspect of artificial intelligence (A.I.) that involves the examination and interpretation of human behavior patterns, actions, and responses in various contexts. In the context of the book title "A.I. Solving Emotional Problems: How Artificial Intelligence Can Help Humans in Emotional Situations and Make Better Decisions," behavioral analysis offers valuable insights into understanding, managing, and responding to emotional challenges. Here's how behavioral analysis contributes to the book's theme:

Identifying Emotional Triggers:

Behavioral analysis enables the identification of emotional triggers situations, events, or stimuli that evoke specific emotional responses in individuals. By analyzing behavioral patterns and contextual factors, A.I. systems can detect correlations between external triggers and emotional reactions, providing insights into the factors that influence individuals' emotional states and decision-making processes.

Detecting Maladaptive Behaviors:

Behavioral analysis helps detect maladaptive behaviors patterns of behavior that contribute to or exacerbate emotional problems and distress. By analyzing behavioral data and identifying deviations from normative patterns, A.I. systems can flag potential signs of maladaptive coping strategies, avoidance behaviors, or self-destructive tendencies, enabling early intervention and support to mitigate adverse outcomes.

Predicting Emotional States:

Behavioral analysis enables the prediction of individuals' emotional states and trajectories based on their behavioral patterns, contextual cues, and historical data. By leveraging machine learning algorithms, A.I. systems can analyze patterns of behavior and identify predictive indicators of emotional states, enabling proactive interventions and personalized support to promote emotional well-being and resilience.

Understanding Decision-Making Processes: Behavioral analysis sheds light on individuals' decision-making processes and cognitive biases that influence their choices and behaviors in emotional situations. By analyzing decision-making patterns, information processing strategies, and emotional regulation techniques, A.I. systems can identify cognitive biases such as confirmation bias, availability bias, and anchoring bias, enabling individuals to make more informed and rational decisions in emotional contexts.

Tailoring Interventions and Support Strategies: Behavioral analysis informs the development of tailored interventions and support strategies that address individuals' unique behavioral patterns, emotional needs, and preferences. By analyzing behavioral data and identifying effective intervention approaches, A.I. systems can customize support resources, coping mechanisms, and therapeutic modalities to match individuals' specific challenges and strengths, enhancing the effectiveness and relevance of emotional support services.

Continuous Monitoring and Feedback: Behavioral analysis enables continuous monitoring and feedback on individuals' emotional well-being and progress towards their emotional goals. By analyzing behavioral data in real-time, A.I. systems can provide timely feedback, reinforcement, and guidance to individuals as they navigate emotional situations and challenges, empowering them to develop adaptive coping skills and resilience over time.

Ethical Considerations and Privacy Protection: In the application of behavioral analysis for emotional insight, it is essential to uphold ethical standards and prioritize user privacy and confidentiality. By implementing robust data anonymization techniques, privacy-preserving algorithms, and transparent data governance policies, A.I. systems can safeguard individuals' sensitive information and foster trust and confidence in the A.I.-human interaction. Additionally, ensuring accountability, transparency, and user

consent in the collection and use of behavioral data is crucial for maintaining ethical standards and respecting individuals' autonomy and dignity.

In summary, behavioral analysis offers valuable insights into understanding, managing, and responding to emotional problems, guiding decision-making processes, and promoting emotional well-being in the digital age. By leveraging the capabilities of behavioral analysis, we can enhance our understanding of human behavior, develop more effective interventions, and create supportive environments that empower individuals to navigate emotional situations with greater insight, resilience, and empathy.

Virtual Reality (VR) and Augmented Reality (AR) for Emotional Therapy

Virtual Reality (VR) and Augmented Reality (AR) are transformative technologies that hold significant promise for enhancing emotional therapy and promoting emotional well-being. In the context of the book title "A.I. Solving Emotional Problems: How

Artificial Intelligence Can Help Humans in Emotional Situations and Make Better Decisions," VR and AR offer innovative solutions for immersive, personalized, and effective emotional therapy interventions. Here's how VR and AR contribute to emotional therapy:

Immersive Therapeutic Environments: VR and AR technologies create immersive, simulated environments that replicate real-world scenarios and experiences. In emotional therapy, VR and AR environments can be designed to evoke specific emotions, trigger memories, or simulate challenging situations, providing individuals with opportunities to confront and process their emotions in a controlled and supportive setting.

Exposure Therapy and Desensitization: VR-based exposure therapy is a highly effective technique for treating phobias, anxiety disorders, and post-traumatic stress disorder (PTSD). By immersing individuals in virtual environments that replicate their feared or triggering stimuli, VR exposure therapy enables gradual desensitization and

habituation to anxiety-provoking situations, empowering individuals to confront and overcome their fears in a safe and controlled manner.

Emotion Regulation and Coping Skills Training: VR and AR platforms can be used to deliver emotion regulation and coping skills training interventions. Through interactive simulations, guided visualization exercises, and biofeedback mechanisms, individuals can learn and practice adaptive coping strategies, relaxation techniques, and mindfulness exercises to manage stress, anxiety, and emotional dysregulation more effectively.

Social Skills Training and Empathy Building: VR and AR experiences offer opportunities for social skills training and empathy building exercises. By simulating social interactions, interpersonal conflicts, and empathetic exchanges, individuals can develop communication skills, perspective-taking abilities, and emotional intelligence in virtual environments, enhancing their capacity for empathetic understanding and constructive interpersonal relationships.

77

Personalized Feedback and Progress Tracking: VR and AR systems can provide personalized feedback and progress tracking features to individuals undergoing emotional therapy interventions. By analyzing user interactions, physiological responses, and emotional cues in real-time, VR and AR platforms can offer tailored feedback, insights, and recommendations to individuals, facilitating self-awareness, insight, and goal attainment in the therapeutic process.

Integration with A.I.-Powered Virtual Assistants: VR and AR technologies can be integrated with artificial intelligence (A.I.)-powered virtual assistants to enhance the therapeutic experience and support individuals in emotional regulation and decision-making. By leveraging natural language processing (NLP) and sentiment analysis capabilities, virtual assistants can engage users in empathetic conversations, offer real-time support, and provide personalized guidance and encouragement in emotional situations.

Ethical Considerations and Privacy Protection: In the development and deployment of VR and AR for emotional therapy, it is essential to address ethical considerations and prioritize user privacy and confidentiality. By implementing robust data encryption, anonymization techniques, and transparent data policies, VR and AR platforms can safeguard individuals' sensitive information and foster trust and confidence in the therapeutic process. Additionally, ensuring informed consent, autonomy, and dignity in the use of VR and AR technologies is crucial for maintaining ethical standards and respecting individuals' rights and preferences.

In summary, Virtual Reality (VR) and Augmented Reality (AR) offer powerful tools for enhancing emotional therapy, promoting emotional well-being, and empowering individuals to navigate emotional situations with greater insight, resilience, and empathy. By leveraging the capabilities of VR and AR technologies, we can create immersive, personalized, and effective therapeutic interventions that harness the transformative potential of artificial intelligence (A.I.) to help individuals address emotional problems and make better decisions in their lives.

Immersive Experiences for Emotional Healing

In the context of the book title "A.I. Solving Emotional Problems: How Artificial Intelligence Can Help Humans in Emotional Situations and Make Better Decisions," immersive experiences offer innovative solutions for emotional healing and well-being. By leveraging virtual reality (VR), augmented reality (AR), and other immersive technologies, individuals can engage in therapeutic experiences that promote emotional awareness, resilience, and healing. Here are several immersive experiences for emotional healing:

Virtual Reality Exposure Therapy:

Virtual reality exposure therapy immerses individuals in simulated environments that replicate real-life situations or triggers associated with their emotional challenges. For example, individuals with phobias or PTSD can confront their fears or traumatic memories in a safe and controlled virtual environment, allowing them to gradually desensitize and process their emotions under the guidance of trained therapists.

Mindfulness and Meditation in Virtual Environments:

VR environments can be designed to facilitate mindfulness and meditation practices, offering individuals serene and tranquil settings to explore and cultivate inner peace and emotional balance. Through immersive guided meditation sessions, individuals can practice mindfulness techniques, deep breathing exercises, and relaxation exercises to alleviate stress, anxiety, and emotional distress.

Virtual Support Groups and Peer Counseling:

VR platforms can facilitate virtual support groups and peer counseling sessions where individuals facing similar emotional challenges can connect, share experiences, and provide mutual support and encouragement. By fostering a sense of community and belonging in virtual environments, individuals can feel validated, understood, and empowered to navigate their emotional journeys with resilience and optimism.

Narrative Therapy and Storytelling in Augmented Reality: Augmented reality experiences enable individuals to engage with interactive narratives and storytelling experiences that reflect and validate their emotional experiences and struggles. By overlaying digital content onto the physical world, AR applications can provide personalized narratives, affirmations, and coping strategies that resonate with individuals' unique emotional needs and perspectives, fostering a sense of empowerment and agency in their healing process.

Art and Creative Expression in Virtual Spaces: Virtual reality environments serve as creative canvases for individuals to express themselves artistically and explore their emotions through various forms of art and creative expression. From painting and sculpting to music composition and dance, VR art platforms enable individuals to channel their emotions, experiences, and aspirations into tangible and immersive artworks, fostering self-discovery, catharsis, and emotional transformation.

Biofeedback and Physiological Monitoring in Immersive Environments:

Immersive experiences can integrate biofeedback and physiological monitoring technologies to track individuals' physiological responses, such as heart rate variability, skin conductance, and brainwave patterns, during emotional healing sessions. By providing real-time feedback on individuals' emotional arousal and stress levels, immersive environments empower individuals to develop self-awareness, self-regulation, and coping skills to manage their emotions effectively.

Empathetic Virtual Companions and Therapeutic Avatars:

Virtual companions and therapeutic avatars powered by artificial intelligence (A.I.) can engage individuals in empathetic conversations, offer emotional support, and provide personalized guidance and encouragement in immersive environments. By leveraging natural language processing (NLP) and sentiment analysis capabilities, virtual companions can adapt their responses and interactions to reflect individuals' emotional states and needs, fostering a sense of understanding, validation, and connection in the therapeutic process.

In summary, immersive experiences offer powerful avenues for emotional healing, self-discovery, and personal growth in the digital age. By harnessing the capabilities of virtual reality (VR), augmented reality (AR), and other immersive technologies, individuals can embark on transformative journeys of emotional healing, empowerment, and resilience, supported by the transformative potential of artificial intelligence (A.I.) to help them navigate emotional challenges and make better decisions in their lives.

Simulated Decision-Making Practice Scenarios

Simulated decision-making practice scenarios provide individuals with opportunities to engage in realistic and immersive situations where they can navigate complex emotional challenges and make informed decisions. These scenarios, tailored to the themes explored in the book "A.I. Solving Emotional Problems: How Artificial Intelligence Can Help Humans in Emotional Situations and Make Better Decisions," aim to enhance emotional intelligence, resilience, and decision-making skills. Here are several examples of simulated decision-making practice scenarios:

Conflict Resolution in the Workplace:

Scenario: You are a manager leading a team project, and two team members are in conflict over different approaches to completing a critical task. The conflict is affecting team morale and productivity.

Decision-Making Practice: Navigate through conversations with each team member individually, gather perspectives, identify underlying emotions, and facilitate a resolution that addresses both parties' concerns while maintaining team cohesion and productivity.

Family Crisis Management:

Scenario: Your family is facing a crisis, such as financial difficulties or a health issue affecting a loved one. Emotions are running high, and different family members have varying opinions on how to address the situation.

Decision-Making Practice: Navigate through family discussions, manage emotions, prioritize needs, and make decisions collaboratively while considering the emotional well-being and perspectives of each family member.

Personal Life Transitions:

Scenario: You are considering a major life transition, such as changing careers, relocating to a new city, or ending a relationship. Each decision carries emotional weight and involves trade-offs.

Decision-Making Practice: Explore the potential outcomes of each decision, weigh personal values and priorities, manage uncertainty and fear of the unknown, and make choices aligned with long-term emotional well-being and fulfillment.

Crisis Intervention and Mental Health Support:

Scenario: You encounter a friend or family member experiencing a mental health crisis, such as severe anxiety or suicidal ideation. You must provide immediate support and connect them with appropriate resources.

Decision-Making Practice: Assess the urgency and severity of the situation, listen empathetically, validate emotions, de-escalate crises, and take decisive actions to ensure the safety and well-being of the individual while respecting their autonomy and dignity.

Ethical Dilemmas in Professional Settings:

Scenario: You encounter ethical dilemmas in your professional role, such as conflicts of interest, whistleblowing situations, or decisions with potential moral implications.

Decision-Making Practice: Analyze ethical considerations, weigh potential consequences, consult relevant guidelines and policies, seek input from trusted colleagues or mentors, and make principled decisions aligned with ethical standards and personal integrity.

Navigating Interpersonal Relationships:

Scenario: You are navigating complex interpersonal dynamics, such as establishing boundaries, managing conflicts, or fostering healthy communication in personal or professional relationships.

Decision-Making Practice: Recognize and validate emotions, communicate assertively and empathetically, negotiate compromises, and set boundaries that prioritize emotional well-being and mutual respect in relationships.

These simulated decision-making practice scenarios offer individuals opportunities to develop and refine their emotional intelligence, problem-solving skills, and decision-making capabilities in diverse contexts. By engaging in realistic and immersive experiences, individuals can build confidence, resilience, and adaptive coping strategies to navigate emotional challenges and make better decisions in their lives, supported by the insights and techniques explored in the book "A.I. Solving Emotional Problems."

CHAPTER 3

CASE STUDIES

Emotion Recognition in Mental Health Screening

Scenario: A mental health clinic integrates artificial intelligence (A.I.) technology for emotion recognition into their screening process. Patients interact with a virtual assistant that uses facial recognition and natural language processing to assess emotional states and identify potential indicators of depression, anxiety, or other mental health concerns.

Outcome: The A.I.-powered emotion recognition system enables clinicians to prioritize patients based on their emotional needs, streamline the screening process, and provide timely interventions and support for individuals experiencing emotional distress.

Virtual Reality Exposure Therapy for PTSD:

Scenario: A military veteran suffering from post-traumatic stress disorder (PTSD) participates in virtual reality exposure therapy sessions. Immersed in virtual environments that simulate combat scenarios and triggering stimuli, the veteran gradually confronts and processes traumatic memories under the guidance of a therapist.

Outcome: Virtual reality exposure therapy helps the veteran desensitize to traumatic triggers, reduce avoidance behaviors, and regain a sense of control over their emotions and reactions. Over time, the veteran experiences a significant reduction in PTSD symptoms and improved quality of life.

Chatbot Support for Anxiety Management:

Scenario: An individual struggling with generalized anxiety disorder (GAD) accesses a mental health chatbot for support and coping strategies. The chatbot employs natural language processing to engage in empathetic conversations,

90

provide relaxation techniques, and offer personalized resources for managing anxiety symptoms.

Outcome: The individual finds solace and validation in interacting with the chatbot, which offers round-the-clock support and practical guidance for navigating anxiety-provoking situations. By incorporating chatbot interventions into their daily routine, the individual experiences improved emotional regulation, reduced anxiety levels, and enhanced overall well-being.

Predictive Analytics for Suicide Prevention:

Scenario: A crisis hotline utilizes predictive analytics algorithms to identify individuals at high risk of suicide based on call data, linguistic patterns, and demographic factors. Trained crisis counselors receive real-time alerts for callers exhibiting elevated suicide risk, enabling proactive intervention and support.

Outcome: Predictive analytics algorithms enable crisis counselors to prioritize and triage callers effectively, assess suicide risk levels, and implement appropriate intervention strategies. By leveraging data-driven insights, the crisis hotline achieves higher rates of successful suicide prevention and provides crucial support to individuals in emotional distress.

Augmented Reality Coping Skills Training for Children with Autism:

Scenario: Children with autism spectrum disorder (ASD) participate in augmented reality coping skills training sessions designed to enhance emotion recognition, social communication, and self-regulation abilities. AR applications overlay interactive visual prompts and social stories onto real-world environments, providing tailored support and scaffolding for emotional learning.

Outcome: Children with ASD demonstrate improvements in emotion recognition, perspective-taking, and coping skills following augmented reality interventions. The interactive and engaging nature of AR technology fosters motivation, engagement, and generalization of skills to real-life social contexts, empowering children to navigate emotional situations more effectively.

These case studies illustrate the diverse applications of artificial intelligence (A.I.) in addressing emotional problems, supporting individuals in emotional situations, and facilitating better decision-making processes. By leveraging A.I.-powered interventions and technologies, individuals can access timely support, personalized interventions, and evidence-based strategies to enhance their emotional well-being and resilience.

Real-World Examples of A.I. Applications in Emotional Problem-Solving

Woebot:

Woebot is a chatbot developed by psychologists and A.I. experts to provide cognitive-behavioral therapy (CBT) interventions for individuals experiencing symptoms of depression and anxiety. Through natural language processing (NLP) and machine learning algorithms, Woebot engages users in supportive conversations, offers personalized coping strategies, and tracks mood patterns to provide real-time feedback and intervention.

X2AI's Tess:

Tess, developed by X2AI, is an A.I.-powered mental health chatbot designed to provide emotional support and intervention for individuals facing various mental health challenges. Tess utilizes sentiment analysis, language processing, and deep learning algorithms to assess users' emotional states, offer empathetic responses, and provide evidence-based interventions to manage stress, anxiety, and depression.

Microsoft's Project InnerEye:

Project InnerEye, developed by Microsoft, is an A.I.-powered tool that assists oncologists in the treatment of cancer patients. By analyzing medical images, such as MRI scans and CT scans, Project InnerEye identifies tumor boundaries, tracks disease progression, and assists clinicians in making treatment decisions. The tool enhances emotional well-being by providing clinicians with accurate and timely information to guide patient care and treatment planning.

Affectiva's Emotion AI:

Affectiva's Emotion AI platform utilizes facial expression analysis and emotion recognition algorithms to understand human emotions in real-time. The technology is used in various applications, including market research, advertising, and driver monitoring systems. By capturing and analyzing facial expressions, Affectiva's Emotion AI provides insights into consumer preferences, emotional responses, and engagement levels, enabling businesses to tailor their products and services to meet customer needs effectively.

Moodbit:

Moodbit is an A.I.-powered employee well-being platform that helps organizations monitor and support employee mental health and emotional well-being. Using sentiment analysis and mood tracking algorithms, Moodbit analyzes employee feedback, surveys, and communication channels to identify trends, patterns, and areas of concern related to emotional well-being in the workplace. The platform enables organizations to implement targeted interventions, foster a supportive work environment, and prioritize employee mental health.

Cognito Therapeutics' Digital Therapeutics Platform:

Cognito Therapeutics develops digital therapeutics platforms that leverage A.I. and neurostimulation technologies to treat neurological disorders, such as Alzheimer's disease and cognitive decline. By combining personalized cognitive assessments, adaptive learning algorithms, and neurofeedback techniques, Cognito's digital therapeutics platform delivers tailored interventions to improve cognitive function, memory retention, and emotional well-being in patients with neurodegenerative conditions.

These real-world examples demonstrate the diverse applications of artificial intelligence (A.I.) in addressing emotional problems, supporting individuals in emotional situations, and facilitating better decision-making processes. By harnessing the power of A.I.-powered interventions and technologies, individuals can access timely support, personalized interventions, and evidence-based strategies to enhance their emotional well-being and resilience.

Mental Health Chatbots

Mental health chatbots represent a promising application of artificial intelligence (A.I.) in providing accessible and personalized support for individuals facing emotional challenges. In the book "A.I. Solving Emotional Problems: How Artificial Intelligence Can Help Humans in Emotional Situations and Make Better Decisions," mental health chatbots play a crucial role in offering empathetic conversations, evidence-based interventions, and practical guidance for managing emotional well-being. Here are several examples of mental health chatbots:

Woebot:

Woebot is an A.I.-powered mental health chatbot designed to deliver cognitive-behavioral therapy (CBT) interventions for individuals experiencing symptoms of depression and anxiety. Through natural language processing (NLP) and machine learning algorithms, Woebot engages users in supportive conversations, offers personalized coping strategies, and provides psychoeducation on cognitive distortions and emotion regulation techniques.

Tess by X2AI:

Tess is an empathetic mental health chatbot developed by X2AI to provide emotional support and intervention for individuals facing various mental health challenges. Tess utilizes sentiment analysis, language processing, and deep learning algorithms to assess users' emotional states, offer empathetic responses, and provide evidence-based interventions to manage stress, anxiety, and depression.

Wysa:

Wysa is an A.I.-powered mental health chatbot that offers emotional support, mood tracking, and self-help exercises for individuals seeking assistance with stress, anxiety, and low mood. Using cognitive-behavioral techniques and mindfulness practices, Wysa engages users in conversational therapy sessions, provides relaxation techniques, and guides users through evidence-based exercises to promote emotional well-being.

Youper:

Youper is an emotional health assistant that combines A.I. with techniques from cognitive-behavioral therapy, mindfulness, and acceptance and commitment therapy. It engages users in conversational therapy sessions, tracks mood patterns, and offers personalized interventions to help individuals manage stress, improve mood, and enhance emotional resilience.

Replika:

Replika is an A.I.-powered chatbot designed to engage users in meaningful conversations, provide emotional support, and foster personal growth and self-discovery. Users can engage with Replika in text-based conversations, share their thoughts and feelings, and receive empathetic responses and reflections that promote self-awareness, emotional expression, and connection.

Talkspace:

Talkspace is an online therapy platform that offers access to licensed therapists and counselors through text-based messaging. While not purely an A.I. chatbot, Talkspace integrates A.I.-driven

99

tools and algorithms to match users with compatible therapists, facilitate communication between clients and therapists, and monitor therapy progress and outcomes.

These mental health chatbots demonstrate the potential of artificial intelligence (A.I.) to provide accessible, scalable, and personalized support for individuals navigating emotional challenges. By leveraging natural language processing, sentiment analysis, and cognitive-behavioral techniques, mental health chatbots empower individuals to access evidence-based interventions, build coping skills, and enhance emotional resilience in the digital age.

Personalized Therapy Algorithms

In the book "A.I. Solving Emotional Problems: How Artificial Intelligence Can Help Humans in Emotional Situations and Make Better Decisions," personalized therapy algorithms play a pivotal role in delivering tailored interventions, addressing individual emotional needs, and promoting effective decision-making processes. These algorithms leverage artificial intelligence (A.I.) techniques to analyze data, identify patterns, and generate personalized treatment plans that align with individuals' unique emotional profiles. Here are several components of personalized therapy algorithms:

Data Collection and Assessment:

Personalized therapy algorithms begin by collecting comprehensive data about individuals' emotional states, behaviors, and experiences. This may include self-reported assessments, mood tracking, physiological data (e.g., heart rate variability), and contextual information (e.g., life events, environmental factors).

A.I. algorithms analyze diverse sources of data to assess individuals' emotional well-being, identify underlying patterns and trends, and detect indicators of emotional distress, such as depressive symptoms, anxiety levels, or stress triggers.

Risk Stratification and Prioritization:

Personalized therapy algorithms stratify individuals into risk categories based on their assessed level of emotional distress, severity of symptoms, and vulnerability factors. Risk stratification algorithms prioritize individuals at higher risk of adverse outcomes, such as suicide risk or acute crisis situations, for immediate intervention and support.

By categorizing individuals based on their emotional needs and level of risk, personalized therapy algorithms ensure that resources and interventions are allocated efficiently and equitably to address the most pressing concerns.

Treatment Matching and Recommendation:

Personalized therapy algorithms match individuals with evidence-based interventions and therapeutic modalities that are most appropriate for their specific emotional needs, preferences, and treatment goals. Treatment recommendation algorithms consider factors such as treatment efficacy, individual preferences, cultural background, and comorbidities.

A.I. algorithms leverage machine learning techniques to analyze treatment outcomes, predict response trajectories, and refine treatment recommendations over time based on individuals' evolving needs and preferences.

Adaptive Intervention Planning:

Personalized therapy algorithms adapt intervention plans dynamically in response to individuals' progress, feedback, and changing circumstances. Adaptive intervention planning algorithms monitor individuals' response to treatment, assess treatment adherence and engagement, and adjust intervention strategies accordingly.

A.I. algorithms incorporate feedback loops and decision rules to modify treatment plans, intensify interventions, or introduce alternative approaches based on individuals' response patterns and treatment outcomes.

Outcome Monitoring and Feedback:

Personalized therapy algorithms track individuals' treatment progress, monitor symptom severity, and evaluate treatment outcomes using standardized measures and assessment tools. Outcome monitoring algorithms provide individuals with personalized feedback on their progress, highlight areas of improvement, and identify potential barriers to recovery.

A.I. algorithms facilitate continuous learning and improvement by analyzing treatment data, identifying predictors of treatment response, and refining algorithmic models to enhance the effectiveness and efficiency of personalized therapy interventions.

Ethical Considerations and Privacy Protection:

In the development and deployment of personalized therapy algorithms, it is essential to uphold ethical standards and prioritize user privacy and confidentiality. Algorithms adhere to principles of data privacy, informed consent, and data security to protect individuals' sensitive information and maintain trust in the therapeutic process.

Personalized therapy algorithms promote transparency, accountability, and user autonomy by providing individuals with clear information about data usage, algorithmic decision-making processes, and the option to opt out or modify their treatment preferences.

A.I.-Driven Emotional Well-being Apps

In the book "A.I. Solving Emotional Problems: How Artificial Intelligence Can Help Humans in Emotional Situations and Make Better Decisions," A.I.-driven emotional well-being apps serve as innovative tools for individuals to access personalized support, develop emotional resilience, and make informed decisions about their mental health. These apps harness the power of artificial intelligence (A.I.) to deliver tailored interventions, monitor emotional patterns, and empower users to navigate emotional challenges effectively. Here are several examples of A.I.-driven emotional well-being apps:

Moodify:

Moodify is an A.I.-driven emotional well-being app that utilizes natural language processing (NLP) and sentiment analysis algorithms to track users' mood fluctuations and emotional states based on their journal entries, social media posts, and conversations.

The app provides personalized insights and recommendations to help users understand their emotional patterns, identify triggers of stress or anxiety, and develop coping strategies to manage their emotions more effectively.

Emotionally Intelligent:

Emotionally Intelligent is an A.I.-powered emotional well-being app that offers interactive exercises, mindfulness activities, and cognitive-behavioral therapy (CBT) techniques to support users in building emotional resilience and enhancing self-awareness.

Using machine learning algorithms, the app adapts its content and recommendations to users' emotional needs, preferences, and progress, offering tailored interventions and guidance for managing stress, improving mood, and fostering emotional well-being.

Mindful Moments:

Mindful Moments is an A.I.-driven mindfulness app that leverages biofeedback and physiological monitoring techniques to guide users through relaxation exercises, deep breathing techniques, and meditation practices.

The app utilizes A.I. algorithms to analyze users' stress levels, heart rate variability, and galvanic skin response, providing real-time feedback and personalized recommendations to help users achieve a state of calmness and emotional balance.

Calm Companion:

Calm Companion is an A.I.-powered emotional support app that offers empathetic conversations, virtual companionship, and personalized interventions for individuals experiencing loneliness, anxiety, or depression.

The app's chatbot interface utilizes natural language understanding (NLU) and sentiment analysis to engage users in supportive conversations, validate their emotions, and provide empathetic responses and coping strategies tailored to their emotional needs.

Headspace AI:

Headspace AI is an A.I.-driven meditation and mindfulness app that offers guided meditation sessions, sleep stories, and stress-relief exercises to promote emotional well-being and mental clarity.

The app integrates A.I. algorithms to track users' meditation habits, analyze their meditation experiences, and deliver personalized recommendations for enhancing mindfulness practice and cultivating a sense of presence and awareness in daily life.

Thrive AI:

Thrive AI is an A.I.-powered mental health and resilience app that provides evidence-based interventions, self-care activities, and peer support networks for individuals experiencing stress, burnout, or emotional challenges.

The app's A.I. engine monitors users' emotional states, social interactions, and activity levels to identify early signs of emotional distress, deliver timely interventions, and connect users with relevant resources and support networks in their community.

These A.I.-driven emotional well-being apps exemplify the potential of artificial intelligence to support individuals in managing their emotional health, fostering resilience, and making informed decisions about their well-being. By harnessing the capabilities of A.I. technologies, individuals can access personalized interventions, receive timely support, and develop sustainable strategies for enhancing emotional well-being in the digital age.

CHAPTER 4

ETHICAL CONSIDERATIONS

In the book "A.I. Solving Emotional Problems: How Artificial Intelligence Can Help Humans in Emotional Situations and Make Better Decisions," exploring the ethical dimensions of using artificial intelligence (A.I.) to address emotional problems is paramount. While A.I. offers immense potential to support individuals in emotional situations and enhance decision-making processes, it also raises significant ethical considerations that must be carefully navigated. Here are some key ethical considerations:

Privacy and Confidentiality:

A.I. algorithms often require access to sensitive personal data, such as emotions, mental health history, and behavioral patterns. It's crucial to ensure robust data protection measures are in place to safeguard individuals' privacy and confidentiality.

Ethical frameworks should prioritize informed consent, transparent data practices, and data minimization principles to mitigate risks of unauthorized access, data breaches, and privacy violations.

Bias and Fairness:

A.I. algorithms may inadvertently perpetuate biases and inequalities present in the data used for training, leading to unfair outcomes and disparities in access to emotional support and decision-making resources.

Ethical guidelines should promote fairness, equity, and transparency in A.I. development and deployment, including rigorous evaluation of algorithmic biases, proactive mitigation strategies, and ongoing monitoring for unintended consequences.

Autonomy and Informed Consent:

A.I.-driven interventions should respect individuals' autonomy, agency, and right to self-determination in managing their emotional well-being and decision-making processes.

111

Ethical frameworks should emphasize the importance of informed consent, voluntary participation, and user control over A.I.-generated recommendations, ensuring individuals have the freedom to accept, reject, or modify algorithmic suggestions based on their preferences and values.

Transparency and Explainability:

A.I. algorithms often operate as black boxes, making it challenging for individuals to understand the underlying decision-making processes, evaluate algorithmic outputs, and hold developers accountable for algorithmic errors or biases.

Ethical guidelines should promote transparency, explainability, and interpretability in A.I. systems, enabling users to comprehend how algorithms work, assess their reliability and accuracy, and make informed choices about their use in emotional situations and decision-making contexts.

Human-A.I. Collaboration:

A.I. should augment, rather than replace, human judgment, empathy, and intuition in addressing emotional problems and making decisions. Ethical considerations should prioritize human-centered design principles, ensuring A.I. technologies complement human expertise and enhance, rather than diminish, the quality of human interactions and emotional support.

Collaboration between A.I. developers, mental health professionals, ethicists, and end-users is essential to co-design ethical A.I. solutions that align with users' needs, values, and cultural contexts, fostering trust, acceptance, and engagement in the therapeutic process.

Accountability and Oversight:

A.I. developers and stakeholders bear ethical responsibility for the design, deployment, and impact of A.I. systems on individuals' emotional well-being and decision-making processes.

Ethical frameworks should establish mechanisms for accountability, governance, and independent oversight of A.I. technologies, including mechanisms for auditing algorithmic decision-making, addressing user grievances, and ensuring compliance with ethical standards and regulatory requirements.

By addressing these ethical considerations, stakeholders can promote responsible and ethical use of artificial intelligence in addressing emotional problems, fostering trust, transparency, and accountability in the development and deployment of A.I. solutions, and ultimately advancing the well-being and decision-making capabilities of individuals in emotional situations.

Privacy Concerns in A.I.-Assisted Emotional Support

In "A.I. Solving Emotional Problems: How Artificial Intelligence Can Help Humans in Emotional Situations and Make Better Decisions," exploring privacy concerns related to A.I.-assisted emotional support is essential. While artificial intelligence (A.I.) holds promise for enhancing emotional well-being and decision-making processes, it also raises significant privacy considerations that must be carefully addressed. Here are some key privacy concerns:

Data Collection and Storage:

A.I.-assisted emotional support systems often rely on extensive data collection, including user interactions, emotional expressions, and personal information shared during therapy sessions or interactions with A.I. chatbots.

Privacy concerns arise regarding the scope and purpose of data collection, the types of data collected, and the duration for which data is stored. Users may be wary of sharing sensitive emotional or personal information if they are uncertain about how their data will be used and protected.

Data Security and Encryption:

A.I.-driven emotional support platforms must implement robust data security measures to safeguard users' sensitive information against unauthorized access, data breaches, and cyberattacks.

Encryption techniques, secure transmission protocols, and access controls should be implemented to protect data integrity and confidentiality, ensuring that user data remains private and secure throughout its lifecycle.

Third-Party Access and Sharing:

A.I.-assisted emotional support systems may involve third-party vendors, service providers, or developers who have access

115

to users' data for system development, maintenance, or improvement purposes.

Privacy concerns arise regarding the sharing, transfer, and access of user data by third parties, raising questions about data ownership, consent requirements, and the potential for data misuse or exploitation.

User Consent and Control:

Users must be informed about the types of data collected, the purposes for which data is used, and the rights they have regarding their personal information.

Privacy concerns emerge when users are not adequately informed about data collection practices, lack transparency regarding how their data is used, or have limited control over the sharing or deletion of their personal information.

Algorithmic Bias and Profiling:

A.I. algorithms used in emotional support systems may inadvertently perpetuate biases or stereotypes based on users' demographic characteristics, emotional expressions, or behavioral patterns.

Privacy concerns arise when A.I. algorithms generate inaccurate or biased assessments of users' emotional states, leading to potential discrimination, stigmatization, or profiling based on sensitive attributes such as race, gender, or mental health status.

Regulatory Compliance and Accountability:

A.I.-assisted emotional support platforms must adhere to relevant privacy regulations, data protection laws, and industry standards governing the collection, use, and disclosure of personal information.

Privacy concerns emerge when organizations fail to comply with legal requirements, lack transparency in their privacy practices, or lack mechanisms for accountability and redress in cases of privacy violations or data breaches.

By addressing these privacy concerns and implementing privacy-enhancing measures, A.I.-assisted emotional support systems can foster trust, transparency, and confidence among users, ensuring that individuals feel empowered to seek support and make informed decisions about their emotional well-being while safeguarding their privacy and data protection rights.

Ensuring Inclusivity and Cultural Sensitivity

In "A.I. Solving Emotional Problems: How Artificial Intelligence Can Help Humans in Emotional Situations and Make Better Decisions," it's crucial to address the importance of inclusivity and cultural sensitivity in the development and deployment of artificial intelligence (A.I.) solutions for emotional support. Recognizing and respecting diverse cultural backgrounds, values, and beliefs is essential for creating inclusive and effective A.I.-driven interventions. Here are key considerations for ensuring inclusivity and cultural sensitivity:

Diverse Representation in Data:

Ensure that A.I. systems for emotional support are trained on diverse datasets that represent a wide range of cultural backgrounds, languages, and social contexts.

Incorporate diverse voices, perspectives, and experiences in data collection, annotation, and model development to mitigate biases and promote cultural inclusivity in A.I. algorithms.

Cultural Competence in Design:

Design A.I.-assisted emotional support systems with cultural competence in mind, considering the cultural norms, values, and communication styles of diverse user populations.

Tailor user interfaces, language preferences, and interaction modalities to accommodate diverse cultural preferences and accessibility needs, ensuring that A.I. systems are inclusive and user-friendly for all individuals.

Language and Translation Services:

Provide multilingual support and translation services to accommodate users who speak different languages or dialects.

Ensure that A.I. chatbots and virtual assistants are equipped with natural language processing capabilities to understand and respond to users' inquiries and emotional expressions in their preferred language.

Cultural Sensitivity Training:

Train developers, designers, and support staff on cultural sensitivity and diversity awareness to foster inclusive design practices and mitigate unintended biases in A.I. systems.

Encourage empathy, curiosity, and open-mindedness in engaging with diverse cultural perspectives and experiences, fostering respectful and culturally responsive interactions with users.

Community Engagement and Co-creation:

Engage diverse communities and stakeholders in the co-creation and evaluation of A.I.-driven emotional support solutions, soliciting feedback, and input to ensure that interventions are culturally relevant, meaningful, and acceptable.

Foster partnerships with community organizations, cultural institutions, and mental health advocates to co-design culturally sensitive interventions, promote user empowerment, and address community-specific emotional needs and challenges.

Ethical Considerations and Equity:

Prioritize ethical considerations and equity principles in the development, deployment, and evaluation of A.I. systems for emotional support, ensuring that interventions uphold human rights, dignity, and social justice.

Advocate for policies and guidelines that promote inclusive design practices, address algorithmic biases, and mitigate disparities in access to emotional support services among marginalized and underserved populations.

By prioritizing inclusivity and cultural sensitivity in the design and implementation of A.I. solutions for emotional problems, we can foster trust, engagement, and positive outcomes for diverse individuals and communities. Embracing diversity and cultural richness strengthens the effectiveness and relevance of A.I.-driven emotional support interventions, empowering individuals to navigate emotional situations and make better decisions in ways that honor their unique identities and experiences.

Potential Biases in A.I. Algorithms

In "A.I. Solving Emotional Problems: How Artificial Intelligence Can Help Humans in Emotional Situations and Make Better Decisions," it's critical to acknowledge and address potential biases inherent in artificial intelligence (A.I.) algorithms used to support emotional well-being and decision-making processes. Biases in A.I. algorithms can arise from various sources, including biased training data, algorithmic design choices, and societal inequalities. Here are some potential biases to consider:

Data Bias:

A.I. algorithms learn from historical data, which may reflect societal biases, stereotypes, and inequalities present in human decision-making processes.

Biased training data can perpetuate and amplify existing biases, leading to unfair treatment, discrimination, and disparities in emotional support interventions and decision-making outcomes.

Algorithmic Bias:

Algorithmic design choices, such as feature selection, model architecture, and optimization criteria, can introduce biases into A.I. algorithms.

Biases may manifest in algorithmic decision-making processes, such as prioritizing certain emotional states or response patterns over others, leading to skewed or unfair outcomes for individuals from marginalized or underrepresented groups.

Representation Bias:

A.I. algorithms may underrepresent or misrepresent certain demographic groups, cultural backgrounds, or lived experiences in their training data, leading to biased and incomplete models of emotional well-being and decision-making.

Representation bias can result in inaccurate assessments of individuals' emotional states, limited understanding of diverse emotional expressions, and disparities in access to tailored emotional support interventions.

Confirmation Bias:

A.I. algorithms may exhibit confirmation bias by reinforcing existing beliefs, assumptions, or stereotypes about emotional well-being and decision-making.

Confirmation bias can lead to algorithmic recommendations that align with dominant cultural norms or social expectations, potentially overlooking alternative perspectives, values, and coping strategies held by individuals from diverse backgrounds.

Feedback Loop Bias:

A.I. systems may perpetuate feedback loop biases by incorporating user feedback and interaction data that reflects biased preferences, preferences, and behaviors.

Feedback loop bias can reinforce existing patterns of emotional expression, response, and engagement, leading to echo chamber effects and limiting opportunities for individuals to explore diverse perspectives and emotional experiences.

Contextual Bias:

A.I. algorithms may fail to account for the contextual nuances, cultural differences, and intersectional identities that shape individuals' emotional responses and decision-making processes.

Contextual bias can result in algorithmic interpretations and recommendations that overlook the complexity and diversity of human emotions, leading to standardized or one-size-fits-all approaches to emotional support and decision-making.

By acknowledging and mitigating potential biases in A.I. algorithms, we can promote fairness, transparency, and accountability in the development and deployment of A.I. solutions for emotional problems. Ethical considerations, diversity awareness, and inclusive design practices are essential for addressing biases, fostering trust, and ensuring that A.I.-driven emotional support interventions benefit all individuals, regardless of their background, identity, or lived experience.

CHAPTER 5

THE FUTURE OF A.I. IN EMOTIONAL PROBLEM SOLVING

In "A.I. Solving Emotional Problems: How Artificial Intelligence Can Help Humans in Emotional Situations and Make Better Decisions," the future of artificial intelligence (A.I.) in emotional problem solving holds immense promise for transforming the landscape of mental health care, emotional support, and decision-making processes. As technology continues to advance and our understanding of human emotions deepens, A.I. stands poised to revolutionize how we navigate and address emotional challenges. Here are several key areas that represent the future of A.I. in emotional problem solving:

Personalized Interventions:

A.I. algorithms will increasingly deliver personalized interventions tailored to individuals' unique emotional needs, preferences, and treatment goals.

By leveraging advanced data analytics, machine learning, and personalized modeling techniques, A.I. systems will identify patterns, predict emotional trajectories, and recommend targeted interventions that resonate with users' emotional states and contexts.

Real-Time Monitoring and Feedback:

A.I.-powered emotional support systems will provide real-time monitoring and feedback, enabling individuals to track their emotional well-being, identify triggers of stress or anxiety, and access timely support and resources.

Wearable devices, sensor technologies, and mobile applications will integrate A.I. algorithms to capture physiological signals, monitor emotional arousal, and deliver personalized feedback and interventions in response to users' emotional states.

Interdisciplinary Collaboration:

The future of A.I. in emotional problem solving will involve interdisciplinary collaboration between A.I. researchers, psychologists, neuroscientists, and mental health professionals.

By integrating insights from psychology, neuroscience, and human-computer interaction, A.I. systems will deepen our understanding of emotional processes, enhance empathy and rapport in human-A.I. interactions, and design more effective interventions for emotional regulation and resilience.

Ethical and Regulatory Frameworks:

As A.I. technologies become increasingly integrated into mental health care and emotional support services, the development and deployment of A.I. solutions will be guided by robust ethical and regulatory frameworks.

Ethical considerations, transparency requirements, and accountability mechanisms will ensure that A.I. systems prioritize user well-being, respect user autonomy, and mitigate risks of algorithmic biases, privacy violations, and unintended consequences.

Global Accessibility and Equity:

A.I. solutions for emotional problem solving will prioritize global accessibility and equity, addressing disparities in access to mental health care and emotional support services across diverse populations and communities.

Culturally sensitive, multilingual, and contextually relevant A.I. interventions will be developed to meet the diverse emotional needs, preferences, and cultural norms of individuals around the world, fostering inclusivity and reducing barriers to care.

Human-A.I. Partnership:

The future of A.I. in emotional problem solving will emphasize the importance of human-A.I. partnership, with A.I. systems augmenting, rather than replacing, human judgment, empathy, and intuition.

Collaborative decision-making models, empathetic chatbots, and virtual support communities will empower individuals to leverage A.I. technologies as tools for self-discovery, emotional growth, and collaborative problem-solving in navigating emotional situations and making better decisions.

In summary, the future of A.I. in emotional problem solving holds tremendous potential to empower individuals, enhance emotional well-being, and foster more informed and resilient decision-making processes. By embracing innovation, ethical principles, and human-centered design, A.I. stands poised to revolutionize how we understand, navigate, and support the rich tapestry of human emotions in the digital age.

Advancements in A.I. Technology

In "A.I. Solving Emotional Problems: How Artificial Intelligence Can Help Humans in Emotional Situations and Make Better Decisions," advancements in artificial intelligence (A.I.) technology play a pivotal role in transforming how we understand, address, and support emotional well-being and decision-making processes. As A.I. continues to evolve, new capabilities and innovations are emerging that hold the potential to revolutionize emotional problem solving. Here are several key advancements in A.I. technology:

Natural Language Processing (NLP):

A.I. technologies equipped with advanced natural language processing capabilities can analyze, interpret, and generate human language with remarkable accuracy and fluency.

NLP enables A.I. systems to engage in empathetic conversations, understand nuanced emotional expressions, and provide personalized support and guidance to individuals in emotional situations.

Machine Learning and Deep Learning:

Machine learning and deep learning algorithms enable A.I. systems to learn from vast amounts of data, identify patterns, and make predictions about individuals' emotional states and decision-making behaviors.

By leveraging neural networks and deep learning architectures, A.I. models can recognize complex emotional cues, infer underlying emotional dynamics, and adapt intervention strategies to meet individuals' evolving needs.

Sentiment Analysis and Emotion Recognition:

A.I. technologies equipped with sentiment analysis and emotion recognition capabilities can analyze text, voice, and facial expressions to infer individuals' emotional states, sentiments, and affective responses.

Sentiment analysis algorithms detect subtle shifts in emotional tone, identify key emotional keywords, and provide insights into individuals' emotional experiences and well-being.

Affective Computing:

Affective computing technologies integrate physiological sensors, facial recognition systems, and behavioral analytics to assess individuals' emotional responses and physiological arousal levels.

By measuring physiological signals such as heart rate variability, skin conductance, and facial muscle movements, A.I. systems can quantify emotional states, track emotional arousal patterns, and deliver personalized interventions for emotion regulation and stress management.

Generative Models and Emotional Agents:

Generative models and emotional agents enable A.I. systems to simulate human-like emotional responses, engage in empathetic interactions, and foster rapport and trust with users.

Emotional agents, such as virtual companions and chatbots, leverage generative models to generate empathetic responses, express empathy, and provide emotional support tailored to individuals' unique emotional needs and contexts.

Personalization and Adaptation:

A.I. technologies enable personalized interventions and adaptive learning experiences that respond dynamically to individuals' emotional states, preferences, and goals.

Personalization algorithms analyze user data, identify patterns of emotional well-being, and recommend tailored interventions, coping strategies, and decision-making tools that resonate with individuals' unique emotional profiles.

133

By harnessing the capabilities of A.I. technology, we can unlock new possibilities for understanding, supporting, and enhancing emotional well-being and decision-making processes. As A.I. continues to evolve, it holds the potential to empower individuals, foster resilience, and promote more informed and effective responses to emotional challenges in the digital age.

Integration with Other Fields: Psychology, Neuroscience, and Artificial Intelligence

In "A.I. Solving Emotional Problems: How Artificial Intelligence Can Help Humans in Emotional Situations and Make Better Decisions," the integration of artificial intelligence (A.I.) with other fields such as psychology and neuroscience holds tremendous potential for advancing our understanding of emotional problems and facilitating more effective interventions. By bridging insights from multiple disciplines, we can develop A.I.-powered solutions that are grounded in scientific evidence, empathetic understanding, and personalized approaches to emotional support and decision-making. Here's how integration with psychology and neuroscience enriches the landscape of A.I. solutions:

Psychological Insights:

Psychology provides a rich theoretical framework for understanding human emotions, cognitive processes, and behavior patterns. By integrating psychological insights into A.I. algorithms, we can design interventions that are informed by evidence-based practices and principles of therapeutic effectiveness.

A.I. systems can leverage psychological theories such as cognitive-behavioral therapy (CBT), mindfulness-based interventions, and emotion regulation techniques to deliver tailored support and guidance for individuals experiencing emotional problems.

Neuroscientific Understanding:

Neuroscience offers insights into the neural mechanisms underlying emotions, decision-making processes, and stress responses. By integrating neuroscientific findings with A.I. technologies, we can develop innovative approaches for measuring, interpreting, and modulating neural activity related to emotional experiences.

A.I.-driven neurofeedback systems, brain-computer interfaces, and virtual reality simulations enable individuals to regulate their emotional states, enhance self-awareness, and cultivate adaptive neural patterns associated with emotional resilience and well-being.

Emotion Recognition and Regulation:

A.I. algorithms leverage advances in affective computing and emotion recognition to detect, analyze, and respond to individuals' emotional cues and expressions in real-time.

By integrating principles of emotion regulation and emotion-focused therapy into A.I.-powered interventions, individuals can learn strategies for managing emotional distress, coping with adversity, and fostering emotional resilience in daily life.

Personality Assessment and Trait Analysis:

A.I. technologies integrate psychological frameworks for personality assessment and trait analysis to generate personalized profiles of individuals' emotional traits, temperament, and coping styles.

By leveraging personality insights, A.I. systems can tailor interventions, recommendations, and decision-making strategies to align with individuals' unique emotional characteristics, preferences, and values.

Behavioral Science and Decision-Making:

A.I. models draw upon principles of behavioral science and decision theory to analyze individuals' decision-making processes, biases, and heuristics.

By integrating behavioral insights into A.I.-driven decision support systems, individuals can receive feedback, guidance, and nudges that promote more informed, reflective, and value-aligned decision-making in emotional situations.

Human-A.I. Interaction and Collaboration:

Psychology and neuroscience inform the design of human-A.I. interaction paradigms that foster empathy, rapport, and trust between users and A.I. systems.

By understanding human emotions, cognitive biases, and social dynamics, A.I. designers can create emotionally intelligent agents, virtual companions, and conversational interfaces that facilitate empathetic communication, active listening, and collaborative problem-solving in emotional situations.

By integrating insights from psychology, neuroscience, and other related fields, we can harness the full potential of artificial intelligence to address emotional problems, support human well-being, and empower individuals to make better decisions in the complex and dynamic landscape of human emotions.

Potential Challenges and How to Address Them

In "A.I. Solving Emotional Problems: How Artificial Intelligence Can Help Humans in

Emotional Situations and Make Better Decisions," several potential challenges may arise in the development and implementation of artificial intelligence (A.I.) solutions for emotional support and decision-making. Addressing these challenges is essential to ensure the effectiveness, ethicality, and sustainability of A.I.-powered interventions. Here are some potential challenges and strategies for addressing them:

Ethical and Privacy Concerns:

Challenge: A.I. systems may raise ethical concerns related to privacy, data security, algorithmic bias, and user consent.

Solution: Develop robust ethical guidelines, privacy policies, and regulatory frameworks to govern the responsible development, deployment, and evaluation of A.I. solutions. Prioritize transparency, user autonomy, and data protection principles to mitigate risks and build trust with users.

Algorithmic Bias and Fairness:

Challenge: A.I. algorithms may perpetuate biases and inequalities present in the data used for training, leading to unfair outcomes and disparities in emotional support and decision-making.

Solution: Implement bias detection algorithms, fairness metrics, and algorithmic auditing processes to identify and mitigate biases in A.I. systems. Foster diversity, equity, and inclusion in dataset curation, model development, and algorithmic decision-making to promote fairness and reduce disparities.

User Engagement and Acceptance:

Challenge: Users may be hesitant to trust or engage with A.I.-powered emotional support systems due to concerns about reliability, effectiveness, and user experience.

Solution: Prioritize user-centered design principles, usability testing, and iterative feedback loops to create intuitive, empathetic, and user-friendly A.I. interfaces. Involve end-users, stakeholders, and domain experts in the co-design and evaluation of A.I. solutions to ensure relevance, acceptance, and adoption.

Interpretability and Explainability:

Challenge: A.I. algorithms often operate as black boxes, making it challenging for users to understand how decisions are made or interpret algorithmic outputs.

Solution: Develop interpretable A.I. models, explainable decision-making processes, and visualization techniques that enhance transparency and interpretability. Empower users with explanations, insights, and contextual information to facilitate informed decision-making and foster trust in A.I. recommendations.

Cultural Sensitivity and Inclusivity:

Challenge: A.I. solutions may lack cultural sensitivity and inclusivity, overlooking diverse cultural norms, values, and expressions of emotional well-being.

Solution: Embed cultural competence training, diversity awareness, and inclusive design practices into the development lifecycle of A.I. solutions. Engage with diverse communities, cultural experts, and stakeholders to co-create culturally sensitive interventions that respect and reflect diverse perspectives, languages, and lived experiences.

Human-A.I. Collaboration and Boundaries:

Challenge: A.I. systems may blur the boundaries between human and machine roles in emotional support and decision-making processes, raising questions about accountability, responsibility, and agency.

Solution: Define clear roles, responsibilities, and boundaries for human-A.I. collaboration, emphasizing the complementary strengths of humans and machines in addressing emotional problems. Foster human-centric design approaches that prioritize human autonomy, empathy, and intuition while leveraging A.I. technologies as tools for augmenting human capabilities and enhancing emotional well-being.

By proactively addressing these challenges and embracing ethical, user-centered, and culturally responsive approaches, we can harness the transformative potential of artificial intelligence to empower individuals, foster resilience, and promote better decision-making in emotional situations. Collaboration, empathy, and continuous learning are essential for navigating the complex interplay between technology and human emotions in the pursuit of well-being and flourishing.

CHAPTER 6

EMPOWERING HUMANS THROUGH A.I.

In "A.I. Solving Emotional Problems: How Artificial Intelligence Can Help Humans in Emotional Situations and Make Better Decisions," the integration of artificial intelligence (A.I.) holds the potential to empower individuals by providing innovative tools, insights, and support systems for navigating emotional challenges and making informed decisions. By leveraging A.I. technologies, we can enhance human agency, resilience, and well-being in the face of emotional difficulties. Here's how A.I. empowers humans:

Access to Personalized Support:

A.I. algorithms analyze vast amounts of data to deliver personalized emotional support tailored to individuals' unique needs, preferences, and circumstances.

By offering personalized recommendations, coping strategies, and interventions, A.I. empowers individuals to explore diverse avenues for emotional growth and self-discovery, fostering a sense of agency and autonomy in managing their emotional well-being.

Enhanced Self-Awareness and Reflection:

A.I. technologies facilitate self-reflection and introspection by providing individuals with insights into their emotional patterns, triggers, and coping mechanisms.

Through interactive feedback, emotion tracking, and journaling features, A.I. tools enable individuals to cultivate self-awareness, recognize emotional trends, and identify opportunities for personal growth and development.

Decision Support and Cognitive Enhancement:

A.I. systems offer decision support tools that help individuals weigh options, evaluate consequences, and make more informed choices in emotionally charged situations.

By leveraging data analytics, risk assessment models, and decision-making frameworks, A.I. enhances cognitive processes, reduces decisional uncertainty, and empowers individuals to navigate complex emotional dilemmas with greater clarity and confidence.

24/7 Availability and On-Demand Assistance:

A.I.-powered chatbots, virtual assistants, and mobile applications provide on-demand emotional support and guidance, offering individuals access to resources and assistance anytime, anywhere.

Through asynchronous interactions, real-time messaging, and automated responses, A.I. platforms extend the reach of traditional support services, empowering individuals to seek help, express emotions, and receive validation and empathy in moments of need.

Empathetic Engagement and Connection:

A.I. technologies emulate empathetic behaviors and social cues to foster genuine connections and rapport with users.

Through natural language processing, sentiment analysis, and emotional intelligence algorithms, A.I. agents engage in empathetic conversations, active listening, and emotional validation, creating a supportive and nonjudgmental space for individuals to express themselves authentically and feel understood.

Continuous Learning and Growth:

A.I. systems adapt and evolve over time, learning from user interactions, feedback, and outcomes to improve the quality and effectiveness of emotional support interventions.

By fostering a culture of continuous learning and iteration, A.I. empowers individuals to experiment, iterate, and refine their emotional coping strategies, resilience-building techniques, and decision-making skills in response to changing circumstances and challenges.

By empowering humans through A.I., we can unlock new opportunities for emotional growth, self-discovery, and well-being. Through collaboration, empathy, and innovation, A.I. technologies serve as powerful tools for augmenting human capabilities, fostering resilience, and promoting flourishing in the complex and dynamic landscape of human emotions.

A Collaborative Approach to Emotional Well-being

In "A.I. Solving Emotional Problems: How Artificial Intelligence Can Help Humans in Emotional Situations and Make Better Decisions," a collaborative approach to emotional well-being harnesses the strengths of both human interaction and artificial intelligence (A.I.) technologies to support individuals in navigating emotional challenges and fostering resilience. By fostering collaboration between humans and A.I., we can create holistic, empathetic, and effective solutions for promoting emotional well-being. Here's how a collaborative approach unfolds:

Human-Centered Design:

Collaborative efforts prioritize human-centered design principles, involving end-users, stakeholders, and domain experts in the co-creation and evaluation of A.I.-powered emotional support systems.

By understanding users' needs, preferences, and lived experiences, human-centered design ensures that A.I. solutions

148

are relevant, intuitive, and responsive to the diverse emotional landscapes of individuals.

A.I.-Augmented Human Support:

A collaborative approach recognizes that A.I. technologies augment, rather than replace, human support systems. A.I. acts as a supportive tool, enhancing human empathy, intuition, and relational skills in emotional interactions.

Human support providers, such as therapists, counselors, and caregivers, leverage A.I. insights, data analytics, and decision support tools to inform their practice, personalize interventions, and strengthen therapeutic alliances with clients.

Empathetic Communication and Rapport:

Collaboration between humans and A.I. fosters empathetic communication and rapport-building in emotional interactions. A.I. systems emulate human-like social cues, active listening, and emotional validation to create a supportive and nonjudgmental space for individuals to express themselves.

149

Through natural language processing, sentiment analysis, and emotion recognition, A.I. agents engage in empathetic conversations, fostering trust, connection, and emotional resonance with users.

Personalized Intervention and Feedback:

A collaborative approach tailors emotional interventions and feedback to individuals' unique needs, preferences, and contexts. A.I. algorithms analyze user data, identify patterns, and recommend personalized coping strategies, resilience-building exercises, and decision-making tools.

Human support providers integrate A.I. insights into their practice, contextualizing recommendations, and interventions based on their clinical judgment, relational skills, and understanding of the individual's emotional journey.

Continuous Learning and Improvement:

Collaboration between humans and A.I. fosters a culture of continuous learning and improvement in emotional support services. A.I. systems adapt and evolve over time, learning from user interactions, feedback, and outcomes to enhance the quality and effectiveness of interventions.

Human support providers engage in reflective practice, supervision, and professional development, integrating A.I. insights into their clinical reasoning, evidence-based practice, and ethical decision-making processes.

Ethical Considerations and Accountability:

A collaborative approach emphasizes ethical considerations and accountability in the development, deployment, and evaluation of A.I. solutions for emotional well-being.

Human support providers uphold ethical standards, professional guidelines, and duty of care responsibilities in their practice, ensuring that A.I.-powered interventions prioritize user safety, confidentiality, and informed consent.

By embracing collaboration between humans and A.I., we can create synergistic approaches to emotional well-being that honor the complexity, diversity, and humanity of individuals' emotional experiences. Through empathy, innovation, and shared responsibility, we empower individuals to navigate emotional challenges, build resilience, and lead fulfilling lives in the digital age.

A.I. as a Tool for Self-awareness and Personal Growth

In "A.I. Solving Emotional Problems: How Artificial Intelligence Can Help Humans in Emotional Situations and Make Better Decisions," artificial intelligence (A.I.) serves as a powerful tool for fostering self-awareness and facilitating personal growth in individuals navigating emotional challenges. By leveraging A.I. technologies, individuals can gain insights into their emotional patterns, triggers, and coping strategies, empowering them to cultivate resilience, develop adaptive behaviors, and foster positive emotional well-being. Here's how A.I. serves as a tool for self-awareness and personal growth:

Insightful Data Analysis:

A.I. algorithms analyze vast amounts of data, including emotional expressions, behavioral patterns, and contextual factors, to generate insights into individuals' emotional experiences and responses.

By identifying trends, correlations, and patterns in the data, A.I. provides individuals with valuable information about their emotional states, triggers, and coping mechanisms, fostering greater self-awareness and understanding of their inner experiences.

Reflective Feedback and Self-assessment:

A.I. systems offer reflective feedback and self-assessment tools that prompt individuals to reflect on their emotions, thoughts, and behaviors in a structured and supportive manner.

Through interactive prompts, journaling features, and self-assessment surveys, individuals engage in introspection, identify patterns of behavior, and gain clarity about their emotional needs and aspirations.

Real-time Monitoring and Feedback:

A.I.-powered monitoring tools provide real-time feedback on individuals' emotional states, helping them track changes, recognize patterns, and manage fluctuations in their mood and well-being.

By monitoring physiological signals, sentiment analysis, and behavioral cues, individuals gain awareness of their emotional arousal levels, stress triggers, and early warning signs of emotional distress, empowering proactive self-care and intervention strategies.

Personalized Recommendations and Interventions:

A.I. algorithms generate personalized recommendations and interventions tailored to individuals' unique emotional profiles, preferences, and goals.

By analyzing user data, contextual factors, and historical trends, A.I. systems suggest tailored strategies for emotion regulation, stress management, and self-care practices that align with individuals' values and priorities.

Goal Setting and Progress Tracking:

A.I.-enabled goal-setting tools help individuals set, track, and evaluate progress towards their emotional well-being goals.

By establishing SMART (Specific, Measurable, Achievable, Relevant, Time-bound) goals, individuals clarify their intentions, monitor their progress, and celebrate milestones, fostering a sense of achievement and motivation for continued growth and development.

Reflective Dialogue and Meaning Making:

A.I. chatbots and virtual assistants engage individuals in reflective dialogue, encouraging exploration of deeper emotional insights, values, and meaning making.

Through empathetic conversations, active listening, and open-ended questions, A.I. agents create a supportive and nonjudgmental space for individuals to explore their emotions, clarify their values, and cultivate a sense of purpose and direction in their lives.

By harnessing the capabilities of A.I. as a tool for self-awareness and personal growth, individuals empower themselves to navigate emotional challenges, cultivate

155

resilience, and embark on a journey of self-discovery and fulfillment. Through continuous learning, reflection, and intentional practice, A.I. serves as a companion and catalyst for individuals' emotional well-being and personal transformation.

Building Trust in A.I.-Assisted Emotional Support

In "A.I. Solving Emotional Problems: How Artificial Intelligence Can Help Humans in Emotional Situations and Make Better Decisions," establishing trust in A.I.-assisted emotional support is paramount to the effectiveness and acceptance of these systems. Trust forms the foundation of meaningful human-A.I. interactions and is essential for fostering engagement, collaboration, and positive outcomes in emotional well-being. Here's how trust can be cultivated in A.I.-assisted emotional support:

Transparency and Explainability:

Transparency in how A.I. systems operate and make decisions builds trust with users. Explainability ensures that users understand why A.I. systems provide certain recommendations or responses.

Providing clear explanations of the capabilities, limitations, and data sources of A.I. algorithms helps users feel informed and empowered in their interactions.

Consistency and Reliability:

Consistent performance and reliability instill confidence in A.I.-assisted emotional support systems. Users should feel assured that the system will consistently deliver accurate and relevant support.

Establishing reliability through rigorous testing, validation, and quality assurance processes helps build trust and credibility in A.I. technologies.

User-Centric Design:

A user-centric design approach prioritizes the needs, preferences, and experiences of users. Designing intuitive interfaces and interactions enhances user confidence and trust in A.I. systems.

Soliciting user feedback, conducting usability studies, and iteratively improving the user experience demonstrate a commitment to meeting users' expectations and building trust over time.

Empathetic and Human-like Interaction:

A.I. systems that demonstrate empathy, emotional intelligence, and human-like interaction foster trust and rapport with users. Emulating empathetic behaviors and active listening promotes a sense of connection and understanding.

Designing A.I. interfaces with conversational agents, expressive avatars, and natural language processing capabilities enhances the perceived warmth and authenticity of interactions, building trust in the system's ability to provide meaningful support.

Privacy and Data Security:

Protecting user privacy and data security is essential for establishing trust in A.I.-assisted emotional support systems. Users must feel confident that their personal information is handled with care and respect.

Implementing robust security measures, encryption protocols, and data anonymization techniques helps safeguard user data and mitigate privacy risks, enhancing user trust and confidence in the system.

Ethical Considerations and Accountability:

Upholding ethical standards and accountability principles reinforces trust in A.I.-assisted emotional support. Users should be assured that the system prioritizes their well-being, autonomy, and rights.

Adhering to ethical guidelines, professional codes of conduct, and regulatory requirements ensures that A.I. technologies are deployed responsibly and ethically, fostering trust and credibility with users and stakeholders.

Transparency in Decision-Making Processes:

A.I.-assisted emotional support systems should be transparent about their decision-making processes and the factors influencing recommendations or interventions.

Providing visibility into how A.I. algorithms analyze data, weigh inputs, and generate outputs enables users to understand and trust the rationale behind the system's actions, fostering a sense of agency and collaboration.

By prioritizing transparency, reliability, user-centric design, and ethical considerations, A.I.-assisted emotional support systems can build trust and confidence among users, empowering individuals to leverage these technologies as valuable tools for enhancing emotional well-being and making better decisions in emotional situations. Trust forms the bedrock of effective human-A.I. partnerships, enabling collaborative efforts to address emotional challenges and promote flourishing in the digital age.

CHAPTER 7

CONCLUSION

In "A.I. Solving Emotional Problems: How Artificial Intelligence Can Help Humans in Emotional Situations and Make Better Decisions," we have explored the transformative potential of artificial intelligence (A.I.) in addressing the complex and nuanced realm of human emotions. From understanding emotional challenges to providing personalized interventions and fostering resilience, A.I. technologies offer innovative solutions to support individuals in navigating emotional situations and making informed decisions.

Throughout this journey, we have witnessed the convergence of technology and humanity, where A.I. serves as a catalyst for empowerment, connection, and growth. By harnessing the capabilities of A.I., individuals have gained valuable insights into their emotional experiences, developed adaptive coping strategies, and cultivated a deeper sense of self-awareness and well-being.

A.I.-assisted emotional support systems have revolutionized the way we approach emotional well-being, offering accessible, personalized, and empathetic interventions that meet individuals' diverse needs and preferences. From mental health chatbots to virtual reality therapy, A.I. technologies have expanded the landscape of emotional support, transcending traditional barriers and reaching individuals in new and meaningful ways.

Yet, with the promise of A.I. comes a responsibility to navigate ethical, social, and cultural considerations with care and mindfulness. As we embrace A.I. as a tool for enhancing emotional well-being, we must prioritize transparency, fairness, and accountability, ensuring that A.I. technologies uphold human dignity, autonomy, and rights.

Looking ahead, the future of A.I. in emotional problem-solving holds boundless opportunities for innovation, collaboration, and impact. By fostering interdisciplinary partnerships, embracing diversity and inclusivity, and placing human values at the forefront, we can harness the full potential of A.I. to empower individuals, strengthen communities, and create a more compassionate and resilient society.

In closing, "A.I. Solving Emotional Problems" invites us to reimagine the intersection of technology and humanity, where A.I. serves as a catalyst for empathy, healing, and transformation. Together, let us embrace the possibilities of A.I. in shaping a future where emotional well-being is accessible, equitable, and empowering for all.

As we embark on this journey, let us remember that the true essence of A.I. lies not in its algorithms or capabilities, but in its ability to amplify the human spirit, nurture connection, and inspire hope in the face of adversity. With compassion, curiosity, and collaboration, we can harness the transformative power of A.I. to unlock new horizons of emotional resilience, understanding, and growth.

Thank you for joining us on this exploration of A.I. in solving emotional problems, and may our collective efforts pave the way for a future where technology and humanity unite to create a world of greater empathy, understanding, and well-being for generations to come.

Recap: A.I.'s Role in Solving Emotional Problems

In "A.I. Solving Emotional Problems: How Artificial Intelligence Can Help Humans in Emotional Situations and Make Better Decisions," we have delved into the multifaceted role of artificial intelligence (A.I.) in addressing the complex challenges of human emotions. Throughout our exploration, several key themes have emerged, highlighting the transformative potential of A.I. in supporting individuals' emotional well-being and decision-making processes:

Understanding Emotional Complexity:

A.I. technologies enable us to delve deeper into the intricate landscape of human emotions, offering insights into the diverse range of emotional experiences, triggers, and responses that individuals encounter in their daily lives.

Personalized Interventions:

By leveraging data analytics, machine learning algorithms, and natural language processing, A.I. facilitates the delivery of personalized interventions and support mechanisms tailored to individuals' unique emotional profiles, preferences, and needs.

Empathetic Interaction:

A.I. systems emulate empathetic behaviors, active listening, and emotional validation, fostering meaningful connections and rapport with users. Through empathetic interactions, individuals feel understood, valued, and supported in navigating their emotional challenges.

Enhanced Decision-Making:

A.I. provides decision support tools that empower individuals to make more informed, rational, and value-aligned decisions in emotionally charged situations. By analyzing data, predicting outcomes, and offering insights, A.I. helps individuals navigate complex decisions with clarity and confidence.

Continuous Learning and Adaptation:

A.I. systems evolve over time, learning from user interactions, feedback, and outcomes to enhance the quality and effectiveness of emotional support interventions. Through continuous learning and adaptation, A.I. remains responsive to users' evolving needs and preferences.

Ethical Considerations and Trust:

Ethical considerations are paramount in the development and deployment of A.I.-powered emotional support systems. Transparency, fairness, and accountability build trust and confidence among users, ensuring that A.I. technologies uphold human dignity, autonomy, and rights.

Collaborative Approach:

A collaborative approach between humans and A.I. fosters meaningful partnerships and shared responsibility in addressing emotional challenges. By combining human empathy, intuition, and relational skills with A.I. technologies' analytical capabilities, we create holistic and effective solutions for emotional well-being.

In essence, A.I.'s role in solving emotional problems extends beyond mere technology; it represents a convergence of empathy, innovation, and human-centered design. By harnessing the transformative power of A.I., we empower individuals to navigate emotional complexities, cultivate resilience, and lead fulfilling lives in the digital age.

As we continue to explore the intersections of A.I. and human emotions, let us remain committed to fostering empathy, connection, and understanding in our quest to create a world where emotional support is accessible, equitable, and empowering for all. Through collaboration, compassion, and innovation, we pave the way for a future where A.I. serves as a catalyst for healing, growth, and flourishing in the human experience.

The Ongoing Evolution of AI and Its Potential Impact on Human Well-being

In "A.I. Solving Emotional Problems: How Artificial Intelligence Can Help Humans in Emotional Situations and Make Better Decisions," the ongoing evolution of artificial intelligence (AI) holds immense promise for transforming the landscape of human well-being. As AI technologies continue to advance, their potential impact on emotional support, decision-making

167

processes, and overall human flourishing becomes increasingly significant. Here's a closer look at the evolving role of AI and its potential implications for human well-being:

Advancements in Emotional Intelligence:

AI algorithms are becoming increasingly adept at understanding and responding to human emotions. Through advancements in natural language processing, sentiment analysis, and affective computing, AI systems can detect subtle nuances in emotional expression and tailor responses accordingly. This evolution in emotional intelligence enables AI to provide more empathetic, contextually relevant support in emotional situations, enhancing human well-being by fostering genuine connections and understanding.

Personalized and Adaptive Interventions:

AI-driven personalization is revolutionizing the way emotional support is delivered. By analyzing vast amounts of data, including user preferences, behaviors, and contextual factors, AI systems can generate personalized interventions and coping strategies tailored to individual needs. This level of customization ensures that emotional support aligns with users' unique experiences and challenges, leading to more effective outcomes and improved well-being.

Predictive Insights and Preventive Measures:

AI-powered predictive analytics enable proactive interventions in emotional well-being. By analyzing patterns and trends in user data, AI algorithms can anticipate potential emotional challenges and recommend preventive measures to mitigate their impact. This proactive approach not only enhances resilience but also empowers individuals to take proactive steps towards maintaining their emotional well-being, ultimately fostering greater levels of psychological resilience and self-efficacy.

Ethical Considerations and Human-Centric Design: As AI continues to play a pivotal role in emotional support and decision-making, ethical considerations become paramount. It is essential to ensure that AI systems uphold principles of fairness, transparency, and accountability,

169

prioritizing human dignity, autonomy, and well-being. Human-centric design approaches place users at the center of AI development, emphasizing empathy, inclusivity, and cultural sensitivity in the design and implementation of AI-powered solutions.

Collaborative Human-AI Partnerships:

The evolution of AI presents opportunities for collaborative partnerships between humans and machines in addressing emotional challenges. By leveraging the unique strengths of both humans and AI, we can create synergistic approaches to emotional support that combine human empathy, intuition, and relational skills with AI's analytical capabilities and scalability. This collaborative model promotes mutual learning, empathy, and trust, ultimately enhancing the quality and effectiveness of emotional support interventions.

In conclusion, the ongoing evolution of AI holds immense potential to positively impact human well-being by revolutionizing emotional support, decision-making processes, and resilience-building efforts. By embracing ethical considerations, human-centric design principles, and collaborative partnerships, we can harness the transformative power of AI to create a future where emotional well-being is accessible, equitable, and empowering for all. As we navigate this journey of innovation and discovery, let us remain committed to leveraging AI as a force for good, fostering empathy, connection, and flourishing in the human experience.

Call to Action: Responsible Development and Utilization of A.I. in Emotional Support

In "A.I. Solving Emotional Problems: How Artificial Intelligence Can Help Humans in Emotional Situations and Make Better Decisions," we have explored the transformative potential of artificial intelligence (A.I.) in revolutionizing emotional support and decision-making processes. As we embark on this journey, it is imperative that we prioritize responsible development and utilization of A.I. technologies to ensure positive outcomes and safeguard human well-being. Here's how we can take action:

Promote Ethical Guidelines: Advocate for the establishment of ethical guidelines and standards governing the development, deployment, and utilization of A.I. in emotional support. Encourage policymakers, industry leaders, and stakeholders to prioritize principles of fairness, transparency, accountability, and privacy in A.I. systems.

Foster Interdisciplinary Collaboration: Foster interdisciplinary collaboration between A.I. researchers, psychologists, mental health professionals, ethicists, and community stakeholders to co-create responsible and inclusive A.I. solutions. By leveraging diverse perspectives and expertise, we can develop A.I. technologies that are culturally sensitive, contextually relevant, and responsive to the diverse needs of individuals and communities.

Ensure Transparency and Explainability: Advocate for transparency and explainability in A.I. systems, ensuring that users understand how A.I. algorithms operate, make decisions, and impact their emotional well-being. Promote the development of user-friendly interfaces and educational resources that empower individuals to engage critically with A.I. technologies and make informed choices about their usage.

Prioritize User Privacy and Data Security:

Advocate for robust data protection measures and privacy safeguards to protect user data from unauthorized access, misuse, and exploitation. Promote the adoption of encryption protocols, data anonymization techniques, and secure data storage practices to mitigate privacy risks and build trust with users.

Empower User Agency and Autonomy:

Empower individuals to exercise agency and autonomy in their interactions with A.I. systems. Advocate for the development of user-centric design principles that prioritize user control, consent, and empowerment, enabling individuals to customize their A.I. experiences and access support services that align with their values and preferences.

173

Promote Research and Innovation: Support research initiatives and innovation hubs focused on advancing the responsible development and utilization of A.I. in emotional support. Encourage collaboration between academia, industry, and civil society to address emerging challenges, identify best practices, and drive continuous improvement in A.I. technologies.

Engage in Dialogue and Advocacy: Engage in dialogue and advocacy efforts to raise awareness about the ethical, social, and cultural implications of A.I. in emotional support. Promote public discourse, community engagement, and stakeholder consultation to foster greater understanding, transparency, and accountability in the development and deployment of A.I. technologies.

By taking collective action to promote responsible development and utilization of A.I. in emotional support, we can harness the transformative potential of A.I. to empower individuals, strengthen communities, and create a more compassionate and resilient society. Together, let us build a future where A.I. serves as a catalyst for empathy, connection, and well-being, fostering a world where every individual can thrive emotionally and make informed decisions in their journey toward fulfillment and flourishing.

www.ingramcontent.com/pod-product-compliance
Lightning Source LLC
Chambersburg PA
CBHW070833250726
48662CB00003B/1207